embroidered
originals

Sue Rangeley
2010

SUE RANGELEY

Contents

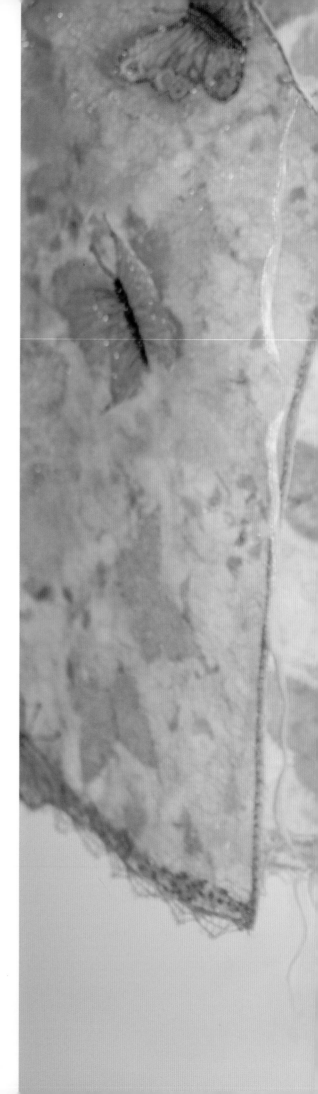

> 'Away with the Fairies'. Embroidered cape.

Symbolic of summer, the winged beauty of butterflies creates a magical flutter across
translucent silk. An ethereal fabric of glistening Angelina is fused with a confetti of silk
butterfly shapes, stitched to white organza. Gossamer layers of chiffon, habutai and iridescent
sheers form the papery wings of the appliqué butterflies. Machine embroidery, beads and
sequins define their delicate patterns in misty pastels touched with metallic sparkle.

Introduction

Embroidery is a timeless art, ever changing, enchanting the eye with stories in fabric and thread. The language of embroidery can stimulate the imagination into expressions of ornate riches or minimal statements. Stitch has the power to stir emotions, inspire dreams and conjure a little magic.

Embroidered Originals takes a journey through my studio creations, sharing landscapes of inspiration and inventive ideas with techniques. Fabric is my blank canvas and fashion textiles emerge as wearable art, touched by the creative possibilities of threads, beads and artful embellishments.

The 'Inspiration' section is a very personal view of my own inspiration(s) in producing the fashion garments displayed. This is followed by a 'Techniques' section showing how the reader might create similar pieces using their own ideas and inspirations.

Artistic expression reflects the changing seasons, evoking an interplay of botanical studies with the textural delights and diversity of embroidery. A visual diary of samples, sketches and fashion textiles reveals nature's unique moments: the frozen beauty of winter, a frenzy of verdant textures in spring, morning mists across English fields, rose romance in my garden, dazzling florals in a summer border, an enchanted walk in ancient woods, autumnal light on a moth's wing.

Embroidery breathes life into fabric surfaces and the art of stitch knows no boundaries.

> 'Vita Alba' (detail). This fichu was made from machine-embroidered Angelina fibres with applied lace flowers.

Inspirations

Winter gardens, transient landscapes of ice, snow and frost, inspire a sequence of ideas for embroidery. Research enriches the creative journey, observation stimulates and is the spark for 'Frost'. Studio 'mood boards' act as a touchstone for design, reflecting key themes that shape the different facets of the stitched surfaces.

The brittle beauty of dormant plants excites the imagination, influencing directions for design. Naked of foliage and colourful petals, organic forms offer a visual resource for texture. Consider:

- bare branch structures
- details of seedheads
- lyrical movements of stems and tendrils
- skeletal laces of decaying leaves.

Touched with the rime of frost, a garden becomes a rich array of icy gems, suggesting myriad themes for embellishment. In contrast, statuesque topiary and an ancient box tree in the artist's garden add bolder drama – dark, velvety evergreens with crisp, clipped leaves. Fragility is the essence of emerging winter flora with swathes of delicate snowdrops, tinted, splashed hellebore petals, aconites and crocus adding a special charm to the frozen wonderland of pattern and texture.

Winter cool dominates the colour palette of 'Frost', exploring a spectrum of seasonal shades. Analysing and observing the changing colours of winter days, from dawn to dusk, leads to recording these with crayon, paint or a collage of paper/fabric colour swatches. The language of colour can be expressed in words – jottings in a 'winter notebook' while observing the garden. Design for embroidery can be sourced from many angles, with words and images interacting to describe colour, texture and form, all recorded on the inspiration board.

Shades of white come naturally to winter landscapes. Imagine the pure white snowflakes, silvery shimmers of ice whites, iridescent, frosted crystallised whites, pearl-white snowdrop petals tinged with green, creams flushed with the pinks and yellows of winter-flowering plants. Each variation suggests a path for selecting paints, fabrics, threads or beads.

Weather patterns dominate wintry skies, inspiring tranquil moods of cool blues, cloudy mauves and greys, the striations of pale watery sunlight and clear sky-blues, broken by the bright sunshine of a sub-zero day. The elements of fog and mist accent the subtle layers of colour transparency to translate into organza sheers. Neutrals can warm up a chilly palette; nature reveals its own paintbox: twiggy taupe, ecru stems, leaf browns, silver-grey bark, grey-green foliage punctuated by spots of berry-brights. All these suggest a rustic, or Nordic, slant for future design schemes.

Drama in inky blacks concludes wintertime 'colour stories'. Think of night skies shot with star sparkle. The finger of Jack Frost highlights further directions for decorative stitch.

∨ A machine-embroidered silver lace fern, wired and beaded with iridescent glass beads.

> Detail of a fabric made using opalescent fused Angelina fibres, machine stitched with sequins.

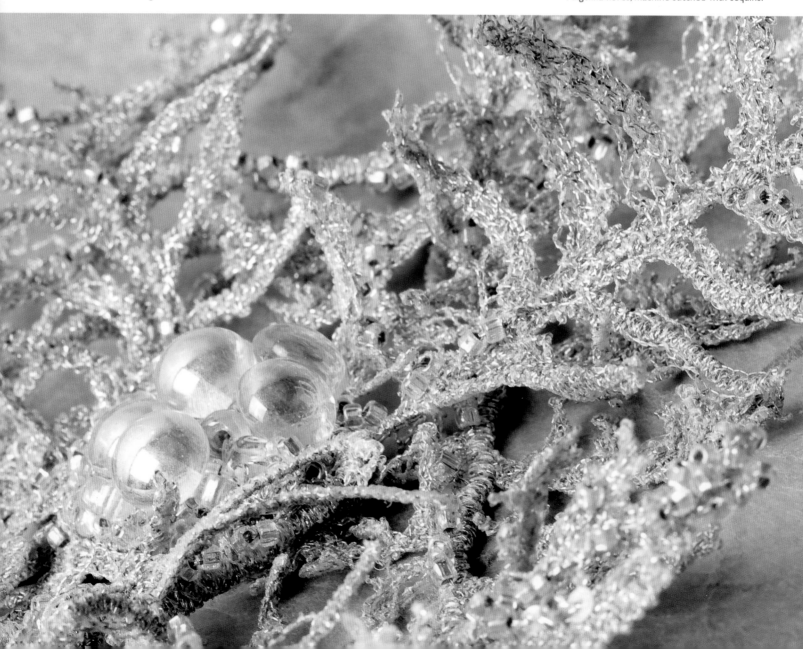

In the studio: *creativity*

The stillness of a Cotswold garden in January has a fresh resonance and plant studies expose winter gardens to closer scrutiny. An artistic eye allows the skeletal, inert plants to enjoy a new vitality as design drawings. Starting with a small sketchbook of inky-black paper, iridescent crayons capture details of plant textures in fleeting, scribbled lines. A splash of interference paint starts a frenzy of seedhead tufts, accented with feathery touches of crayon. Mark-making is intuitive, expressive, abstract – a springboard of ideas for design and stitch.

Scale adds a challenge in drawing with the need to consider proportion and composition. Using large sheets of dramatic black pastel paper can set the stage for plant patterns, coaxing the energy of drawing in random arrangements (see drawing, page 6). Free networks of criss-crossing lines suggest structures for embroidered lace or movements of quilted stitching. Metallic crayons evoke the 'sugar-crystal' trail of hoarfrost on spiky leaves and tendril tangles. Sketches define 'colour-stories' of silvers, mother-of-pearls, opals. Embroideries (see 'Night Frost' samples for evening bodices on page 26–27), are born out of paper doodles – a 'eureka' moment as paint lustre touches black paper, inspiring surface embellishment.

Design studies, too, observe the unique beauty of hellebores, their splashed, spotted, dappled flower faces highlighted as pastels on dark papers – a winter flower worthy of the embroiderer's imaginative needle.

Drawing is a vital ingredient of the design process which heightens perception and unleashes countless wonderful ideas for decorative fabric surfaces. Plant studies provide a portfolio of source material to influence the 'Frost' collection. The embellished fabrics do not follow the imagery in the original drawings precisely, but pursue their spirit into stitch.

∧ Sketchbook studies of plants in winter.

v Dried Eryngium flowerheads.

In the studio:
interpretations

The words *crystalline*, *pearlescence* and *opalescence* express the patina of the 'Frost' samples, stimulating choices of iridescent, metallic threads, silk organzas and tulle, silver lamés, shimmering foils, glass beads and sequins. The sewing machine, combined with fabrics and threads, makes an early appearance, and drawings evolve. Stitch and sketch work in harmony to realise concepts, and the original mood boards are a critical reference for selecting materials, refining colour stories and testing techniques.

Stitch samples play with sketchbook ideas, freely inventing surfaces with fabric manipulation or experimenting with materials such as Angelina. Embellishment has no boundaries and 'Frost' textiles develop organically through playing with abstract ideas and then nurturing specific themes. Tranquillity and transience influence samples, finding expression in the fragile fashion pieces.

Traditional techniques combine with innovation to give embroidery a rich repertoire to explore. Delving into textile archives can empower the art of the needle to pursue new horizons. The exquisite beauty of lace is referenced in the embroidered stomachers on pages 16–19 which look to the artistry of guipure lace, using machine stitch on dissolvable film to create a delicate, icy mesh. Samples of filigree lace drive a vision for bridal fashions, connecting a sketch of a decaying leaf to vintage lace. Past and present entwine to inspire a contemporary embroidery.

Sampling deliberately takes a fresh focus by introducing new fabrics and processes and exploring a new perspective for enhancing fashion. 'Glacial' (right) reinvents the basics of cut-out lace ignoring fussy decoration. Cool, pure, translucent silk organzas move with an elegant flow and are used to style cutwork fabrics for wraps and scarves (see sketch opposite).

Just as sketches act as a catalyst for stitch effects, materials too perform unique magic tricks to seduce the eye. Angelina's fine fibres, full of glitz and sparkle, are a natural choice for 'Frost'. The samples of fused Angelina form a tangled veil of frosty threads for the fichu (pages 20–21). Foiling can offer metallic dazzle, with black silk giving added drama for iridescence, and dark palettes contrasting with snow-white purity.

The 'Night Frost' samples (pages 26–27) give an immediate fashion context by referencing corsetry and couture techniques such as seaming, piping, edgings and lacings, which give new dimensions to stitched, foiled surfaces.

Interpretation through samples breathes life into studio inspiration/mood boards, and fashioning fabrics with stitch moves them into shape and structure. Functional or fantastical, the 'Frost' collection reveals another story with creative stitch.

< Sketches for 'Glacial' and 'Drift' fashions.

> 'Glacial'. Detail of lace organza stole.

∧ 'Frosted Flora'. Machine-embroidered lace in metallic threads with glass crystal and pearl beaded centre.

> 'Ice'. Manipulated appliqué sheers, stitched to foiled silk.

'An erring lace...'
Machine-embroidered stomacher

This embroidery creates an intricate tracery of frosted threads and evokes fashion memory. Historic dress influences shape, and fleeting sketches of frozen plants direct the spirit of the exquisite stitchery. A love poem by Robert Herrick (1591–1674), 'Delight in Disorder', reveals the sensuous nature of dress, throwing the imagination back to another era.

The richly decorated stomachers which captivated Herrick in the 17th century – 'An erring lace which here and there enthralls the crimson stomacher' – offer contemporary stitch an intriguing shape to explore. The V-shaped bodice panels, with intimate associations of *décolletage*, appear first in the 16th-century fashion of open robes. Bodice adornment continues for another two centuries with embroidery, quilted textures, lacing details and metallic trims. For me, the poet's lyrical words sparked an idea to reinvent a stomacher as a surface of pure iridescent, stitched lace. Fragile threads of openwork echo the frozen plant surfaces. Techniques of guipure (machine-embroidered lace) express the essence of the frosted patterns while harking back to the past.

Here, winter whites are tinged with pale greenish glints of the snowdrop to create a palette of iridescent machine threads. Starting with a patterned sketch of free-flowing lines, the sewing machine translates the design into a glistening mesh. Sensitive use of scale releases rhythmic movements of intertwined stems in textured stitching, contrasting delicate networks of threads with dense stitched, corded effects.

The stomachers of the 17th century tantalised the eyes with a high sparkle factor, with added precious stones and pearls. This contemporary descendant accents embroidered lace with opalescent appliqué, studded with frosted glass beads. Stitched edges are left unresolved and irregular; as with any fragment of old lace, precision would not be appropriate.

STUDIO TECHNIQUES:

Machine lace	page 87
Appliqué sheers	page 81
Beadwork	page 82

< Machine-embroidered lace stomacher and detail inset.

∧ Sketch of frozen plant heads.

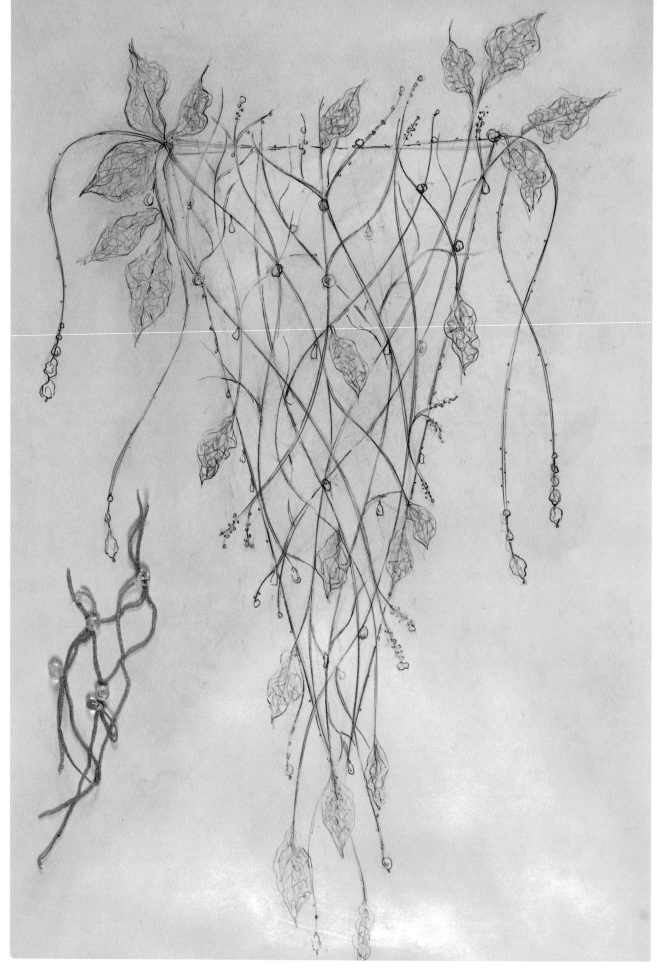

∧ Pencil and wash sketch with sample for embroidered lace stomacher.

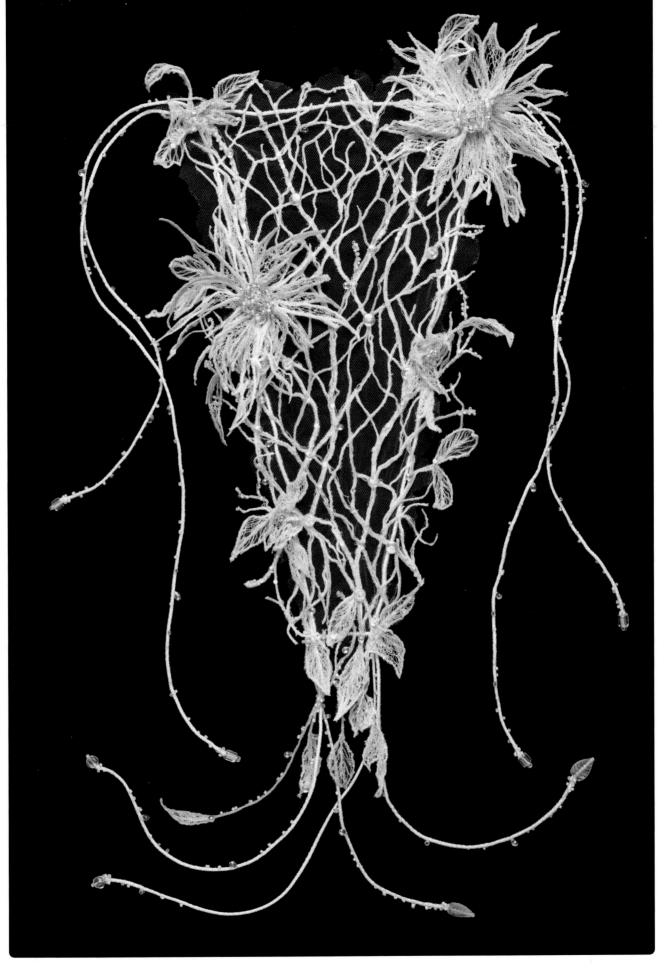

∧ Stomacher panel for bridal dress. Machine-embroidered lace on silk tulle.

'Vita Alba'
Embroidered fichu

For this garment, the spirit of nature fashions a fabric. Winter hedgerows, veiled in frosty tangles of wild clematis, create an ornamental spectacle of pattern to inspire stitch. Ethereal trails of gossamer textures and beadwork sparkle on fused fibres to enhance fashion. Embroidery enters the world of Narnia, conjuring wisps of frippery to cloak cool shoulders.

The colour palette embraces winter chill. Here, opalescent whites mingle with cool metallic shades: aqua blues, mint greens, watery blue-greys and the blue-mauves of winter skies. A luminous warmth of pale sunlight flickers across this fichu, using the iridescence unique to Angelina fibres.

Creative embroidery thrives on free experimentation, and modern materials are a catalyst for stimulating new techniques. The opaline mesh which evolves through fusing layers of sparkly, synthetic Angelina fibres provides the magic of a cobweb – a fabric appears 'out of thin air'. Techniques drive vision, combining fashion concepts to reinvent a rambling plant as a glistening fichu. Stitch spontaneously scribbles across the fused surface in fine lines of shimmering threads, imitating the movements of twisted tendrils with kinks, loops and curlicues. Intuitively, artistic imagination follows the free spirit of machine embroidery, shaping a fabric

to grace a fashion. No measured pattern structure here – a style emerges with natural movement, a swaying of draped shimmer, sprinkled with tiny sequins.

The distinctive textures of 'old man's beard' or 'traveller's joy' (wild clematis) are a dream for embellishment. Adorned with a hoarfrost, the crystallised climbers reflect the glassy glints of beads. A mélange of lacy flora enhance the wispy fichu. Machine embroidery and hand beading intermingle to give 'iced sweeties' stitched to perfection. Radiating filaments of machine stitch echo the shape of stamen tassels, feathery seedheads and frozen leaf curls. Intricate trickles of sparkle – pearls, crystals and frosted glass – cling to the fragile web of fibres. Fanciful additions create flickers of opalescence as the gossamer web encircles the shoulders. Frosted beauty freely roams fashion's world, inspiring embroidery with a naturalistic touch.

STUDIO TECHNIQUES:

Angelina fibres	page 80
Frost flower	page 87
Beadwork	page 83

23

'Drift'
Cut-out organza lace

The influence of winter landscapes continues, creating a glacial flow of cutwork sheers. Transparency and translucence achieve the bare simplicity of ice, using white silk organza to develop samples. Fabric manipulation adopts a softer touch – femininity follows the fluid rhythms of sheers with a swish of 1930s bias-cut fabrics.

Shivering ribbons of sliced organza descend in filmy layers as movement and manipulation explore opacity. Shapes that begin as delicate tissue-paper cut-outs finish as meanders of bias silk. Embroidered stitch keeps a minimal profile, accenting the edges with a precise zigzag, in stitches of twinkling iridescence. Beads detail icy glints along the floaty edges – a moving drift and fall of glass droplets.

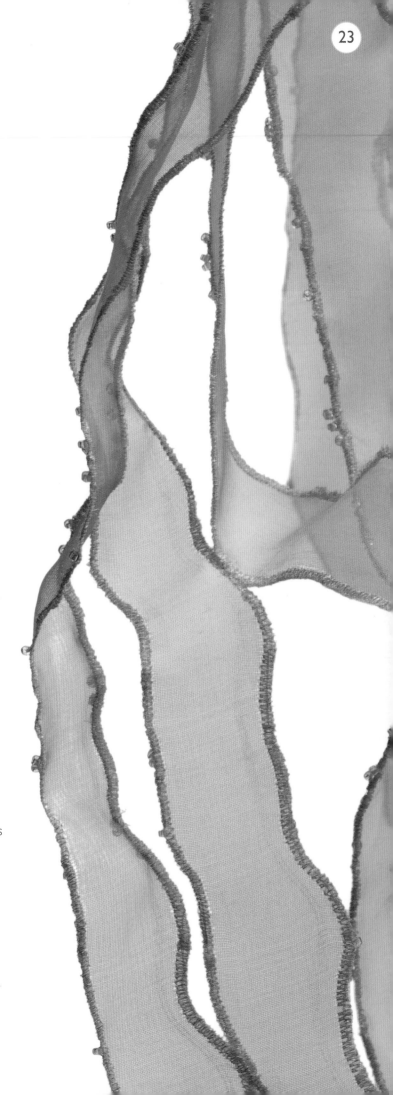

STUDIO TECHNIQUE:

Cut-out lace	page 85

Manipulated organza

This design looks to the frozen horizons of distant lands, extracting ideas to inspire fabric manipulations. Contours and cavities and shifts and drifts of icy waters are visual references for samples of surface relief – dimensions to challenge the artful needle.

Silk organza mirrors the glassy opacity of ice, metallic foils introduce a silver patina, while reflective glacé layers begin the textural changes. Free-motion quilting offers exciting possibilities for stitch improvisation, naturally highlighting the undulating patterns of land and water. Backgrounds of silvered foil, burnished to silk, are a playground for free machine quilting. Stitches of silver thread freely pierce the fabric layers, creating wavy drifts of embossed sparkle.

Hand manipulation contrives a flounce of translucent organza to give convoluted arrangements of frozen ripples on silvery shimmer. Decorative satin stitch, boldly machined in silver twist thread, accents the relief rhythms of the edges. A single sample releases a sequence of ideas for embellishment.

STUDIO TECHNIQUES:

Manipulation	page 90
Decorative edging	page 85
Foiled silks	page 86

'Winter Garden'

The drama of black influences a mood change for 'Frost' embroidery. A drawing of winter plant structures plays a pivotal role, giving depth and substance to samples. Inky-black papers make a decorative ground for mark-making with metallic crayons.

> Stitches of pearlescent thread portray a scribble cluster of daisy heads, pursuing a lacy pattern. Delicate snow-capped seedheads, caught in a web of frost, change into tenuous thread structures. Embroidery deftly explores transient details of nature and lace evolves to shape a fashion story.

> A botanist's eye for detail mingles with the embroiderer's inventive art. Distorted twists of Eryngium's spiky foliage re-emerge as fragments of botanical lace. Meandering lines of straight stitch describe leaf veins, while satin stitch accents the silhouettes of pointed petals. Iridescent threads blend with metallic blues, echoing crayon marks and the plant's inherent colouring. Suspended in a web of Angelina, stitch creates fragile textures, enriched with frosted beads.

> Free expression extracts the essence of dormant bracts, creating patterns of silver thread. Stitchery invents flower forms – a complex radiating structure in silver lace. Repetitious circular movements of machining form dense stitch spots, contrasting with a finer tracery of lines. Winter garden plants turn into silvery laces.

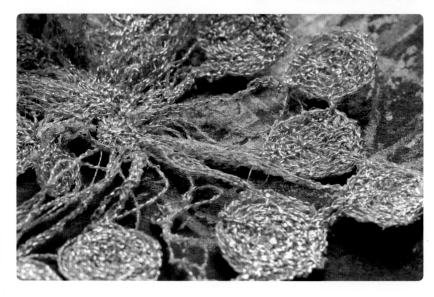

STUDIO TECHNIQUE:	
Machine lace	page 87

> 'Winter Garden Flora' (detail). Crayon on paper.

'Night Frost'
Evening bodice panels

After-dark designs are nurtured by the spirit of the 'Winter Garden' sketch. Frosted crystalline surfaces and winter night skies translate into ink-black silks enhanced with iridescent sparkle. Couture details and costume archives influence and contextualise embellishment. Techniques look to the era of laced bodices, and the art of corsetry invites a creative eye to study seaming, fastenings and edgings. Research embraces a diversity of references.

Lustres of burnished, bonded foils dance across the silk, echoing the spiky Eryngium sketches and the twisted foliage of winter plants. Abstract iridescent shapes and leafy patterns share the reflective drama – fabric interprets the luminous sparkle of frost.

Fashioning the decorative fabrics follows progressive stages, with an interplay of sketchbook, stitch samples and toile shapes. Inspirations for 'Night Frost' also referenced fashion drawings of corselets and basques in *Harper's Bazaar* magazine 1957: sensual shapes of classic 1950s corsetry with shapely seaming, stitched inserts, structured waspies, lacy trims and frills. The figure-defining panels reveal starting points for fashion design and stylish stitching.

Evocative shimmers of metallic foiling are enriched with free machine quilting. Random lines of metallic stitching intermingle, highlighting the dupion silk surfaces with a subtle brocade of textures. Stitched samples, as shown, are used to develop fabrics for bodice panels; decorative quilting creates surface interest within curvaceous shapes.

Finishing touches of rouleau loops, lacings, fancy bows and sheer ruffles serve to contrast meticulous couture-crafted processes with the *joie de vivre* of freely embellished silks. Precision insertions of twirling rouleaux, beaded with dark turquoise crystals, playfully suggest a bodice detail. Functional rouleau loops are reinvented as trimmings.

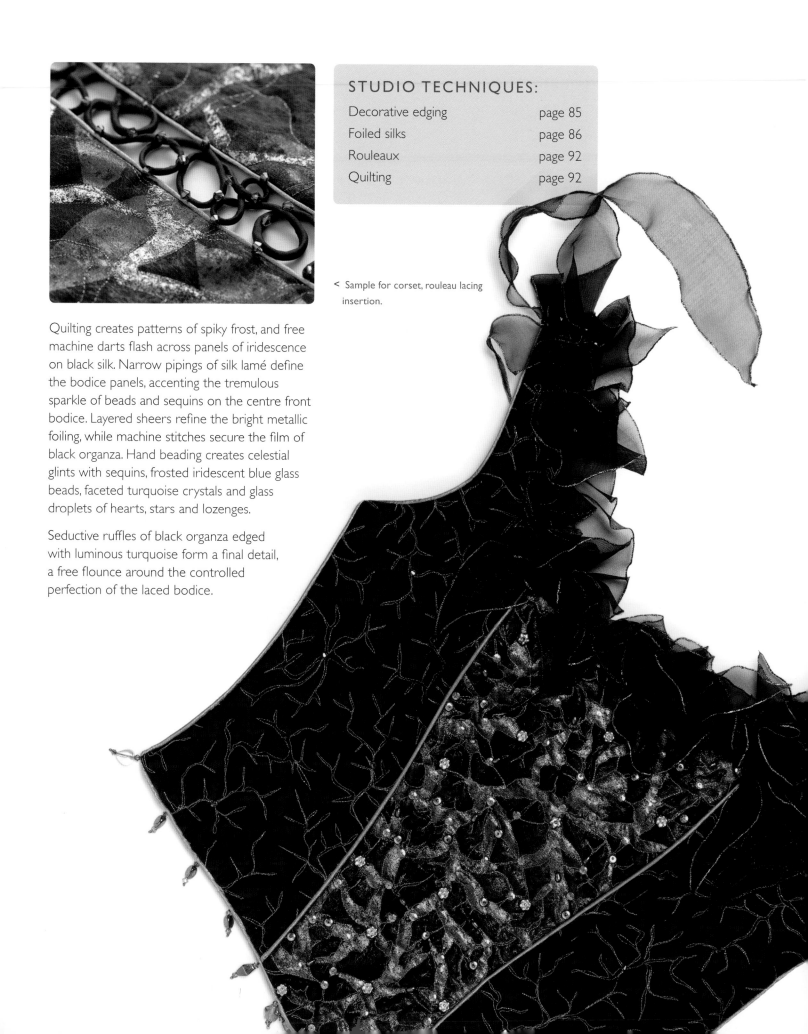

< Sample for corset, rouleau lacing
insertion.

Quilting creates patterns of spiky frost, and free machine darts flash across panels of iridescence on black silk. Narrow pipings of silk lamé define the bodice panels, accenting the tremulous sparkle of beads and sequins on the centre front bodice. Layered sheers refine the bright metallic foiling, while machine stitches secure the film of black organza. Hand beading creates celestial glints with sequins, frosted iridescent blue glass beads, faceted turquoise crystals and glass droplets of hearts, stars and lozenges.

Seductive ruffles of black organza edged with luminous turquoise form a final detail, a free flounce around the controlled perfection of the laced bodice.

Inspirations

In this chapter, the power of green resonates through embroidered fabrics and Mother Nature inspires a path for decorative stitch. English gardens emerging from winter sleep give a fresh context for exploring plant patterns. Seasonal changes map a creative journey – spring into summer – and foliage entices the senses with a diversity of leafy shapes and delicious tints of the green scene.

Memories of a country childhood fuel a passion for green, with vistas of fields, trees and hedgerows catching the imagination and influencing directions for embroidery. The studio recreates this verdant landscape with swathes of silk reflecting different hues, from misty pale peppermint into sharper acidic shades, via sage, fern and grass greens.

Inspiration leads to investigation:

- A box of threads invites a closer analysis of foliage variegation.
- Trays of beads accent green iridescence through sparkling glass and sequins.
- Fabric paints translate subtle shifts of hazy spring-morning greens or rain-washed shades.

Studio pinboards are a movable feast of design references, a creative backdrop which maintains the vitality of source material. Surrounding the senses with the visual and tactile ingredients from the foliage theme is a deliberate choice. The studio becomes a garden of fabrics, threads, plant paintings and pressed leaf collections; the greens of the foliage formulate design ideas.

Two gardens with contrasting settings form the design basis for the embroidered fabrics, establishing a path for samples. The intimacy of my own garden nurtures energetic stitched patterns and my gardening passions drive the design into elaborate lace fashion fabrics. Green symbolises growth and vitality, expressing the zest of spring and summer. Plants are picked, observed and translated into stitch by machine embroidery, catching the immediacy of climbing, scrambling summer stems. Themes dictate the creative interpretation and techniques, with no set rules or boundaries – 'Viridis Lace' (pages 36–37), for example, is a journey of pure intuition and experiment.

The second garden, Glendurgan in Cornwall, inspired a more reflective approach for 'Primavera' sheers on pages 34–35. Quieter echoes of greens with misty, silvery, pearly tints, flow through painted appliqué fabrics. The delights of this garden, lying in a beautiful valley close to the Helford River, suggests so many ideas for embroidery; the essence of 'Primavera' draws on this dreamy, watery setting and the observation of foliage patterns. Here, green finds expression in painterly palettes of sprayed fabrics and design is drawn from pages of pressed flora, reinventing botanical specimens as drifting collections of appliqué sheers.

Foliage offers pattern possibilities. Leaves, often overlooked in favour of colourful flowers, have infinite varieties which stimulate fresh interpretations for fashion or stitched surfaces for interiors. Green is Nature's colour, balanced and harmonious, a reassuring shade to refresh, accent or overwhelm decorative stitch. A desirable fashion colour to rival classic black, a green renaissance resounds through fabric and thread.

In the studio: *creativity*

Artistic expression follows a painterly path, realising the quintessence of the Cornish garden where gauzy veils of mist subdue the lush foliage into hazy green palettes. Soft, tranquil, serene tints are recreated with fabric paints, capturing exact blends through careful mixing, followed by testing on silk swatches. Techniques such as airbrushing or spraying the paint create gentle layers of pale greens across silk habutai and *crêpe de chine*. Watercolour shades merge into surfaces of ivory silk. Spray-painted silks can themselves inspire textile designs. Like a collage of tissue paper, painted silks are shaped into delicate foliage cut-outs, inspired by the pressed leaves.

The inspiration of the foliage theme observes shape, texture and colour in close proximity; the direct experience of plant forms tantalises the eyes. Analysing the green hues of flourishing foliage inspires the selection of machine threads. Creating notebooks of swatches (fabric, paper, paint) triggers memories of shades observed and words can also capture the zest of springtime foliage: fresh lime, soft fern, cool peppermint, glossy green, acid green, mist, grey green, goblin green. The essence of plant movements, leaf shapes and textures is expressed in botanical sketches, before embroidery. Drawing extracts the energy of an unfurling fern, and free pencil sketches dance over a surface of sprayed, sponged paint textures on watercolour paper, suggesting a pattern of stitched lace. Researching and recording the vibrant interplay of leafy exuberance empowers the design direction of stitched textures.

Selecting materials is an essential facet of the design process, together with drawing and collating source information. Draping lengths of silk reveals their potential as fashion fabrics, highlighting options of embroidery and embellishment. A pearly dew-drop shade of silk satin suggests a filmy shimmer for under-stitched lace, suitable for slinky slip dresses. Gauzy green sheers, satins and dupion silks expand the fabric range for fashion. A tailor's stand allows design to explore new dimensions, by freely testing fabric drape and placement of embroidery, while a sketchbook of fashion doodles acts as a diary of ideas for samples. Creativity pursues numerous avenues, embracing a broad canvas of fabrics and techniques, generating original concepts for design.

> Sketch of ferns and mosses in pencil and wash.

The foliage patterns for 'Viridis' lace were stitched on hot-water-soluble voile.

In the studio: *interpretations*

Creativity opens the door of opportunity for interpretation, a crossroads of choices for developing and refining both design and embroidery techniques.

Crayons are now replaced by silky rayon machine-embroidery threads to illustrate a lavish story of spring foliage. Sometimes a vision for a textile design is so vivid that it requires no intermediate sampling stage and, guided only by a whimsical fashion sketch, the embroidery takes a literal plunge into the undergrowth for the 'Viridis' design. Techniques of machine-embroidered lace or *guipure* express the frenzy of spring green foliage. Verdant hues in the threads create a textural language for embroidery, while the soft viscose properties of rayon suit the drape and movement of a wearable fabric.

Fashion drawings capture the free spirit of the green growth with sketches on spray-painted papers, or iridescent green washes tinting backgrounds. Ideas explore complex foliage patterns for skirts and irregular lacy hemlines for strappy tops or diaphanous layers of bonded appliqué. Designs are stepping-stones towards a final creation, playfully exposing the possibilities for embroidery. The 'Primavera' sketch (overleaf) interplays botanical drawings with fashion sketches, indicating placements and scale variations for embroidery. Large plant drawings on tracing paper are also superimposed on garment shapes, revealing further directions for patterns of stitch and appliqué.

'Viridis' followed its organic nature, with the foliage patterns styled by serendipity. Here, speed and skilful free machine embroidery make the interpretation. A single meandering stem of convolvulus leaves diagonally dissects the skirt panel in a fine layer of stitched green organza. Tracings of leaves or drawings on water-soluble voile echo the random spirit of fern fronds and whorls of leaves. Stitch then defines the shapes in different densities of texture across the skirt panel. The sewing-machine needle stitches as freely as pencil on paper, highlighting the rhythms of rampant foliage. Experience and experiment intertwine to shape and structure these foliage textiles. 'Primavera' and 'Viridis' pursue two paths, suggesting options for fashion embroidery ideas.

'Primavera'
Fashion samples and sketch

Springtime foliage veiled in morning dew influences a gentle watercolour palette of misty greens. The ethereal beauty of an emerging season finds expression in appliquéd organza.

The atmosphere of a Cornish garden, with its sweeping vistas of river and secret paths to secluded shorelines, is the context for botanical studies of springtime foliage. A green palette of fabric paints is inspired by the lush vegetation of ferns and hazy shades of the landscape setting, each shade observed and carefully mixed. Translating the subtle misty layers of soft greens onto silk surfaces is naturally expressed with airbrushing, capturing the subtle variations of delicate greens and layering colours to create deeper tones. A collection of watercolour silks, painterly surfaces of *crêpe de chine* and habutai are the appliqué materials for 'Primavera'.

The spectacular scale of the garden at Glendurgan originally inspired an interior textile 'Spirit of the Place – Glendurgan', an airy organza curtain of appliqué plant specimens. A filmy two metre length of silk was reinvented as a diaphanous wrap, inspiring a sequence of wearable fabrics. Concepts for interior design interplay with fashion styles to realise directions for decorated sheers. There are endless possibilities:
- voluminous long kimono coats
- swirling skirts
- enveloping wraps and shawls
- circular capes.

Layering sheers over silky linings provides a contrast for the tailored lines of narrow skirt or sheath dresses.

STUDIO TECHNIQUES:	
Airbrushed fabrics	page 80
Appliqué sheers	page 81

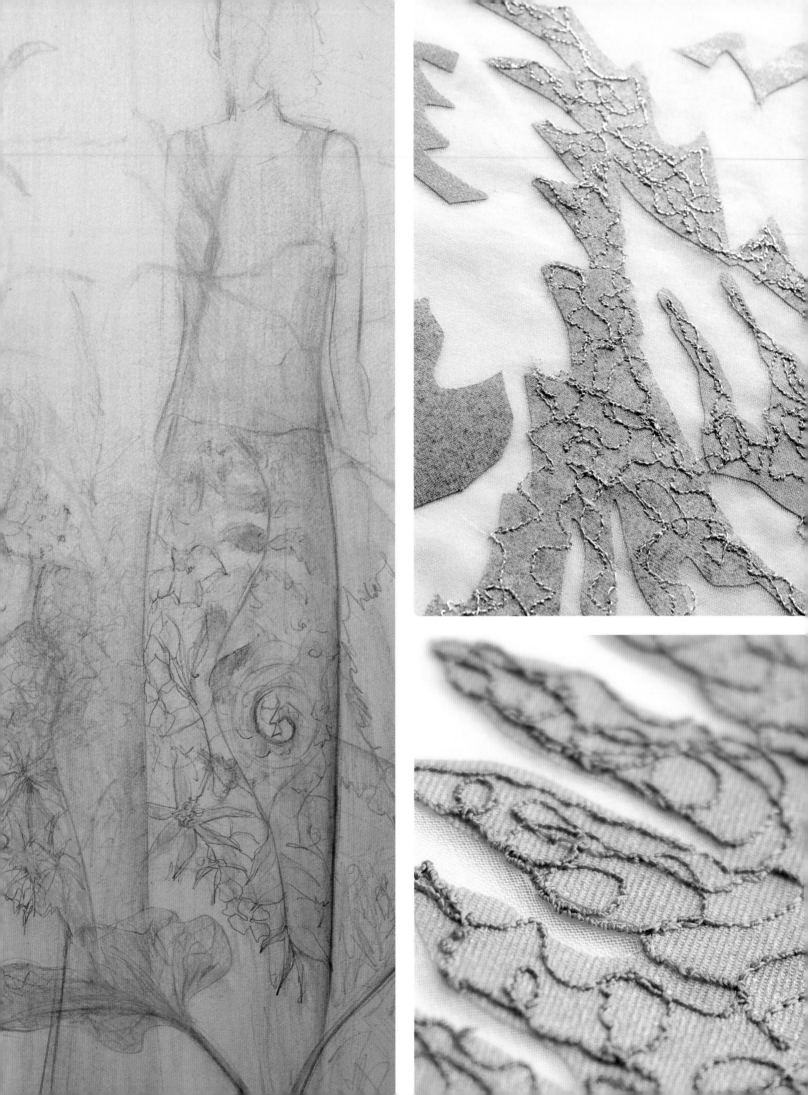

▲ In this study of lacy foliage, silky rayon threads highlight subtle variegations of green shades via experimental machine embroidery which is as versatile as a paintbrush. A network of lacy foliage with interlocking tendrils and filigree spaces could form a bodice, ramble over sleeves or add intriguing details to a dress.

'Viridis'
Machine-embroidered lace skirt panel

Embroidery celebrates green, indulging in a frenzy of lacy textures. A wild corner of a garden resurfaces as finely crafted stitched lace. Surpassing the tranquillity of 'Primavera', embroidery now reflects the lively hues of spring/summer foliage. Flourishing plants display vivid varieties of cool greens which all create a lively thread palette. Consider sharp, acidic limes of Euphorbia, glossy evergreen fern fronds, Helleborus greens, mossy shades of creeping foliage, citrus striations of variegated leaves, pale fern-dappled bluish-greens, spring-green sprigs and shoots plus accents of yellow/green.

These translate into spools of silky machine threads, ready to create chlorophyll splashes across a water-soluble fabric. Threads, like paint pigments, are intermixed, blended and overlaid and machine embroidery gives full expression to luxuriant greens. A pattern of embroidered lace begins with a network of green organza appliqué. Trailing Convolvulus leaves form bold, curvaceous movements across the water-soluble voile. Machine embroidery highlights the details of veins and dense meanders of stitch define rhythmic stems. Energetic embroidered patterns of leaves, sprigs, bracts and tendrils develop freely around the first appliqué layer. Random juxtapositions of foliage patterns move within the skirt panel dimensions. Spontaneously, the designs are sketched on water-soluble voile in preparation for stitchery. Pure thread creates the lace while free machine embroidery textures the foliage shapes in various ways. Simple straight stitch performs a repertoire of linear patterns, filling the leafy shapes while observing the botanical details of the original plants.

> Machine-embroidered leaf shapes were straight stitched in this detail. Silky viscose threads in shades of foliage green give a painterly mix.

STUDIO TECHNIQUE:

Machine lace   page 88

∨ 'Hedera' collection. Evening bag.
Silk velvet background, applied decoration:
beadwork, appliqué, manipulated bias ribbon.

'Forest'
Inspirations

A walk in the woods leads foliage themes into a dramatic mood touched with the dark mystery of dense forest – a contrast to the paler palettes of the spring/summer foliage collections. We escape the garden to explore a wilder diversity in deciduous woodlands, leafy glades and pine forest trails where green mesmerises the senses with infinite variety. Nature captivates the eye with the green splendour of fern, moss, lichen, leaf, branch and bark to unveil a darker side. Light and shade play a part, with tree shadows and silhouettes introducing a dark mystery in shades of black, charcoal and smoke grey; a note of gothic romance pervades the verdant hues.

The remains of an ancient forest surrounds countryside close to my studio, its trees are talismans of past centuries. A mingling of history and nature marks a route for design where references to Victorian black lace can interplay with observations of forest foliage. The secrets of a forest floor carpeted with plants, the moss, leaves and branches inspire a sequence of themes for fabric manipulation and textures in 'Glade'. Woodland foliage intrigues and teases tenuous ideas into designs for accessories (photo right). Tangled thickets spark sketchbooks of spiky lace-like designs for stitch. Hedera helix, the ancient ivy with its heavy foliage and sombre hue, plays a pivotal role in forming fashion shapes and adornments in the 'Hedera' embroideries.

Swathes of green fabrics evoke the foliage palettes in sheers, hand-painted metallics, matt crepes and lustrous velvets. The addition of black, in silk tulle and organza, creates dark, shadowy veils to interplay with the greens.

STUDIO TECHNIQUES:

Appliqué sheers	page 82
Beadwork	page 82
Painted fabrics	page 91
Manipulation	page 90

'Forest'
Themes

Magical woodlands shape a vision for fashion embroidery, directing design down a naturalistic path and nurturing samples into the dimensions of dress and accessories. The themes define the essence of the 'after dark' collections for 'Foliage', intertwining nature with vintage references, to style a mode of mystery.

The 'Enchanted' collection takes the shades of oak, ash, beech and sycamore as inspiration for a collection of scarves, wraps and capes. The pure beauty of green organzas translate the subtle nuances of leafy layers and machine appliqué captures the intrinsic qualities of leaves.

'Sylva' intertwines a magical mix of references to inspire fashion embroidery. Here Victorian black lace, Arthur Rackham's fairy illustrations and the foliage of a forest floor inspire machine-embroidered lace samples, layered over forest green silks. Simple plant and foliage patterns emerge as greenish-black lace in stitched rayon threads. These decorative laces could accent a dress with fancy edgings and trimmings, or create delicate, embroidered lace webs to drape over foliage greens for slinky evening wear.

< 'Enchanted'. Silk organza stole with decorative appliqué leaves, metallic gold stitching and sequins,

The remaining themes are shown on the following pages:

- 'Hedera', the ivy theme generates numerous fashion ideas, from the simple naturalistic design interpretations of glossy green appliqué foliage, through the complex climbing stems, tendrils and roots which form creation and structure of a garment. The exquisite botanical details are hidden in sombre foliage, ready to translate into elaborate encrusted beadwork for belts, basques and bodices.

- 'Glade' places textural and fabric manipulation in focus, developing a collection of surfaces for fashion accessories. 'Foliage' themes look to the intricacies of moss and lichen and broaden embroidery technique and application with another repertoire of stitch effects, thanks to the embellisher machine and machine-made chain stitch. These experimental samples are set to explore more inventive applications for functional form.

- 'Out of the Shadows' introduces a mood of darker mystique, adding black sheers into the greenwood palette. The design translates foliage as silhouettes and shadows at dusk. Layered sheer fabric with stitching mixes black, charcoal and green silk organza to create shadowy tones with accents of green. Markings can be added to foliage appliqué with stitch or paint. The enveloping fashions of capes, cloaks and wraps are explored in sheers, but also suggest directions for velvets or wool crepes.

These themes offer a tantalising array of interpretation for the embroiderer's art. Embroidery, bewitched by a woodland setting, is given free rein to experiment and embellish fashion.

∨ 'Sylva' (detail).
Embroidered lace in rayon and metallic thread was beaded with peridot.

'Hedera'
Rouleaux lace bodice
with choker neckline

Hedera helix inspires embroidery from botanical themes, enriched with a fusion of Victoriana and evocative images of ancient woodland. The ivy's mystique and symbolism are influenced by classical connections with a Grecian origin, naturalistic patterns and vibrant, intense palettes of green.

The original sketch of the ivy plant immediately provoked decorative ideas for embroidery. Nature styles patterns of rampant stems and clinging tendrils, together with fibrous roots and ornamental umbels of flowers and dark berries. Here the design departs from glossy foliage to focus on the sinewy rhythms of ivy growth and dense details of flower and berry clusters. Open linear structures contrast with the embossed medallion motifs and fashion designs express the 'wild thing' persona of the free-spirited ivy.

Fabrics, threads, beads and braids extract *Hedera*'s rich shades of blackish-green and purple-black. The berry-black and dull green colours are enlivened by sparks of acidic yellow-green. The distinctive foliage of the ivy species introduces additional mixes, for other colour stories – splashes of greeny-gold, blotched greens and creamy whites, variegations of silvery tints and purplish bronzes. The 'Hedera' bodice explores the darker spectrum of charcoal and grey-green with the sheen of a metallic lamé fabric. Poison-green sequins add a splash of sparkle.

The techniques of the 'Hedera' samples combine craft traditions and inventive processes. A marriage of past and present encircles creativity in many of the ideas. Victorian collars of Battenberg lace and black lace, beaded with jet, inspire directions for rouleau lace structures. Flights of fantasy follow designs for embellished basques of ornamental berry beadwork in a patina of vintage jet. Curvaceous stems form a

bodice of lace rouleaux, sparkling with sequins and Swarovski crystals. The halter-neck style, influenced by 1970s fashion, has added notes of Victoriana, with an elaborate choker fastening of beadwork and looped rouleaux.

Branches of ivy become a luxurious mix of embroidered and embellished surfaces. Fashion shapes emerge (see sketches on the next page) and textile creations evolve, here a drape of rouleau lace, there a beaded basque or the flowing textures of a belt. Magically, *Hedera helix* inspires the embroiderer's art.

STUDIO TECHNIQUES:

Rouleaux	page 93
Beadwork	page 82

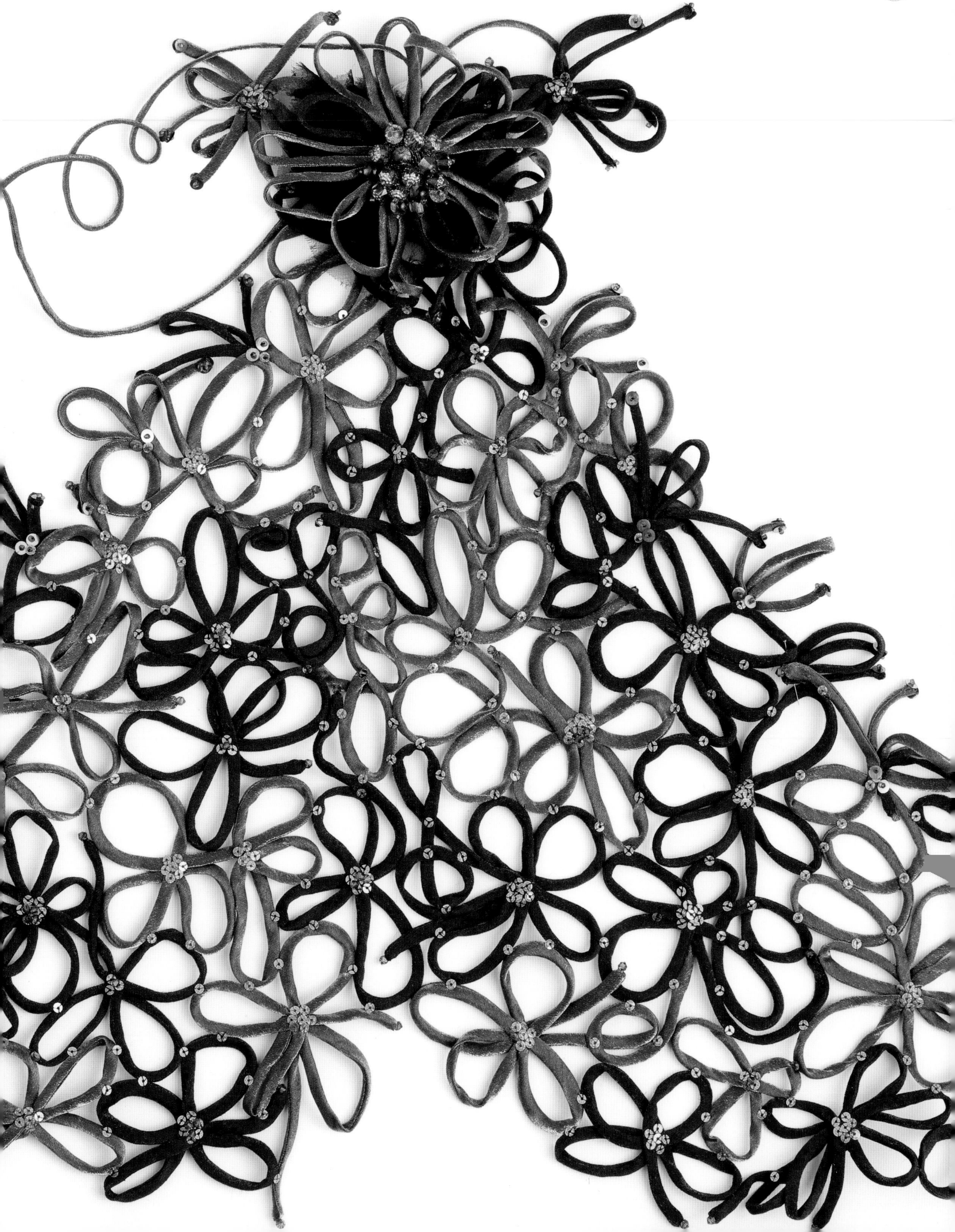

∧ 'Hedera' collection. Sketches for belts, basques and bodices.

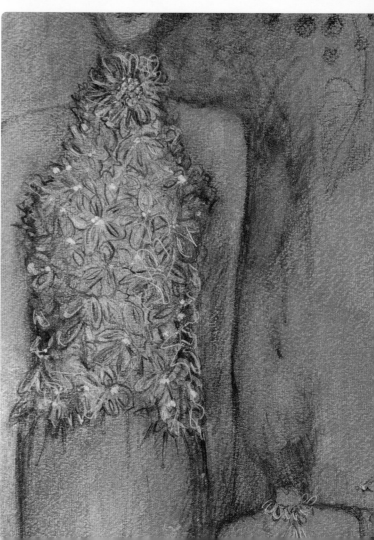

Belt embellishment. Manipulated bias ribbons and wire were beaded with peridot.

'Hedera'
Embellished belt

A painterly sketch of ivy explores the foliage of the species. An iridescent, metallic paint, sponged over the leaves, lifts the evergreen plant with a splash of green-gold and moves the design towards embellished textures of beadwork and fabric manipulation.

The rhythmic twists and turns of the scrambling ivy plant suggest designs for entwining belts, close-fitting basques, bodices and corset creations - the plant's natural structure influencing fashion form. As with the 'Hedera' lace bodice (pages 42–43), it is the movement of stems, clinging to tree bark or creeping across a forest floor, that sparks the ideas for belts. Naturalistic foliage is erased from the design and the focus is moved to botanical details of umbellate berry clusters and the sinewy lines of stems. Intermixed with the ivy theme are textures and shapes from a hawthorn hedge, enriching the palette with bright, berry-like highlights.

Slender machine-stitched wired cords and twiggy tangles of wired silk rouleaux, in green and gunmetal lamé, shape the belt. Embossed medallions of beadwork nestle in wired ruffles of sheers or metallic lamés; radiating seed-heads of machine embroidery add another dimension. Berry-bright beadwork encrusts knotted rouleaux.

STUDIO TECHNIQUES:

Beadwork	page 82
Beaded cords	page 84
Rouleaux	page 92
Wired ruffles	page 91

'Glade'
Samples for embellished accessories

The dappled light of a leafy glade illuminates woodland textures. A verdant carpet of mosses and lichen-coated surfaces inspire the stitched and manipulated samples shown here.

Moss-like crayon patterns on black paper organically translate the intricacies of moss foliage, suggesting ideas for stitch. The heavily textured central area of this small pendant purse uses a space-dyed silk cord, unravelled and machine couched - an undulating mossy cushion of threads (see opposite, bottom). The embroidery evokes the relief surfaces of 17th-century sweet purses. Lichen is more fungi than foliage, a member of the moss family. Its structure is a perfect design source for stitch. The embellisher machine is ideal for interpreting the velvety piles of its textures (see Studio Techniques page 86).

Machine embroidery creates a fantasy adornment for a petite purse (see opposite, top left). Lichen's amazing acidic green and gold shades strike a radiating plant pattern as a frenzy of free stitchery. The exotic berries of the arum, an elusive woodland plant, inspires an embellishment finale: a flash of scarlet Swarovski crystals embossing a silky sheen of poison-green cord.

A chain stitch meander of gold thread, on hand-coloured glade-green organza, makes a moss-like creeping trail. Furrowing and gathering manipulate the sheer silk (see opposite, top right).

STUDIO TECHNIQUES:

< Sweeping marks of greenish, gilded iridescent paints on black organza evoke shafts of sunlight piercing a leafy canopy. The gleam of sequins, attached with tiny green glass beads, enhances the drama of a forest fabric.

'Out of the Shadows'
Capelet

As delicate as a moth's wing, a capelet of organza creates an ethereal cloak of mystery to grace 'after-dark' fashions. The shadowlands of woods translate the dark dimness of twilight hours into the dusky transparency of black silk organza. A ghost of a fabric gives a magical aura of shadowy intrigue and captures the ambience of barely-there shapes in the woods.

Rich forest greens fade into the background, leaving a solo black sheer to express patterns of leafy silhouettes at dusk. Dark silks are enlivened with decorative edgings of serrated leaves, painted with metallic fabric paints in shimmering accents of greenish-gold iridescence. Flickers of sparkle encircle the hemline of the capelet, like dancing fireflies, together with minuscule jet-black sequins and green crystals.

The simple capelet expresses a transient moment with an ethereal flutter of appliqué leaves, and a slender pair of rouleaux makes a minimal ribbon tie for the neckline.

Capes fall naturally from the shoulder, offering embroidery infinite scope. From sheer wisps of stitchery on delicate silks, stitched laces, or bolder creations on velvets and wools, voluminous shapes give total freedom for expression. Elsa Schiaparelli's capes (1938–39) featured highly elaborate designs, inspired by classical themes: Medusa, Apollo, startling wonders of goldwork and beadwork which explode across the backs of evening capes.

Victoriana lurks in the background, inspiring embroidery and fashion shapes. Ornate lace and passementerie are simplified to achieve contemporary elegance.

A glimpse of old lace inspires a machine-embroidered lace with black rayon and green metallics (see page 41). Referencing, but not replicating, the past via costume and fashion collections is a rich resource for design. Vintage textiles infuse designs with interesting cross-references. The 'Out of the Shadows' research took a lace cape from a fancy-dress trunk and reinvented it as gothic glamour, 21st-century style. Fashions for 'after-dark' come out of the shadows, enriched by stitch.

STUDIO TECHNIQUE:

Appliqué sheers page 82

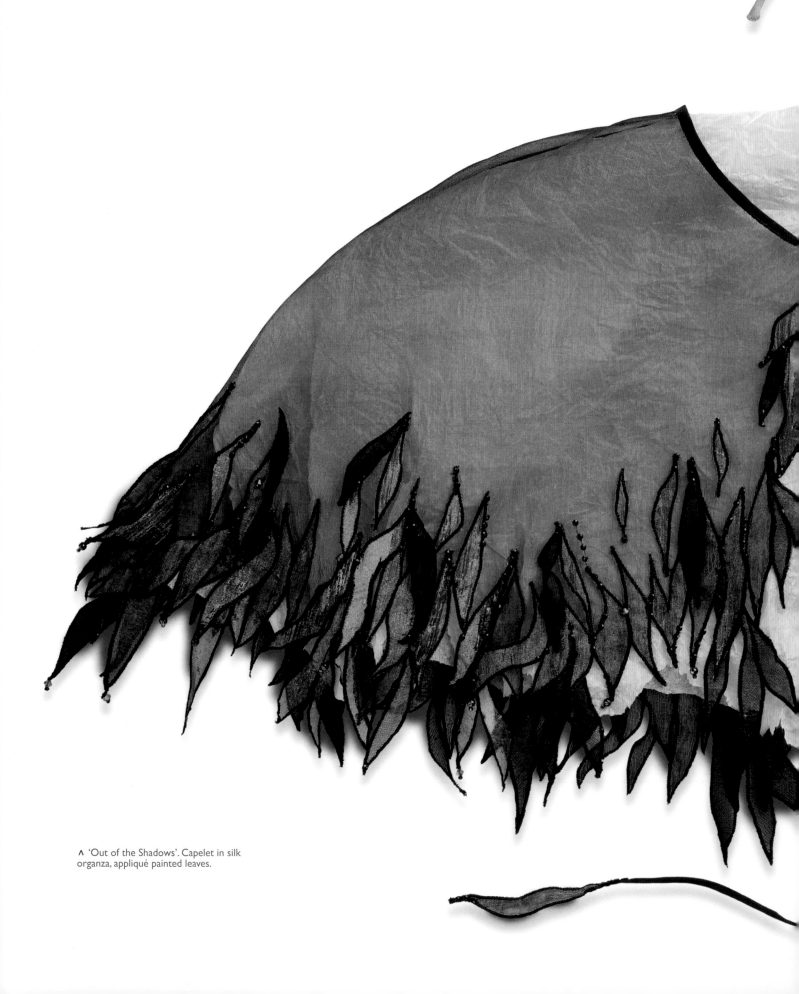

∧ 'Out of the Shadows'. Capelet in silk
organza, appliqué painted leaves.

CHAPTER 3

FLORA

Inspirations

Once again embroidery takes a pleasure path through English gardens, this time inspired by a 'flower power' paradise that stirs the senses and captivates the imagination. Verdant themes hypnotised the 'Foliage' collection, and 'Flora' now embraces an array of blooms. Studio research is a fusion of themes, from botanical archive studies and flower drawings to a Rococo version of rose romance. We'll have dahlia dazzle with a Latino twist and find historic dress mingling with petal charm. The studio is a point of synthesis, as before, structuring ideas from visual references, sketchbooks, plant paintings, museum studies and fashion shapes. When needle and thread touch fabric, flora gives *carte blanche* for creative embroidery.

Design ideas are first generated by the herbarium in a study of the roots of botany, taking a magnifying glass to the complexities of flower forms. Browsing ancient herbals, researching plant collectors' folios or touching pressed-flower specimens leads to the analysis of intricate flora. A personal collection of early 19th-century botanical engravings of Linaeus classifications inspires 'Botanical Reticules' (pages 62–63). Science and art intermingle to create quirky botanical purses.

Inspirations

A bouquet of inspiration for the flowers in 'Flora'
selects some summertime favourites, with the allure
of the rose dominating embroidered surfaces. Old
Bourbon roses, ramblers and the luxuriant climbers
that adorn my garden walls are the subject of delicate
botanical paintings. In the 'Roses Study', watercolour
crayons, delicate washes and subtle pencil marks
interpret the buds, blooms, sprays, leaves and seedheads
as dancing arrangements of pastel petal formations.
Showy dahlia heads, in complete contrast, are sketched
with pastels on black paper, to emphasise the flash and
fizz of their Mexican origins. Across centuries, the art of
botanical illustration has expressed a passion for plants,
these connections inspiring further thought for 'Flora'.
From the jewelled presence of flowers on gilded vellum
manuscripts of the 12th century and the rare blooms
of 17th-century Dutch flower painters to the floral
beauty of the artists Le Moyne, Redouté and Bauer,
all is inspiration. In the studio, portfolios of my flower
paintings suggest designs – the plant portraits ready to
embrace embroidery.

Fashion has always been a fan of flowers. Studio
inspirations peruse fashion archives, conjuring ideas
from source material, while 'mood boards' act as
catalysts for samples, fashion designs or accessory
patterns. Historic paintings can also stimulate
ideas: the famous Botticelli *Primavera* (1458) shows
Flora's flower-strewn costume, suggesting delicate
ethereal appliqué using sheer silks. The Elizabethans
flaunted floral excess in dress and, in the 1930s, Elsa
Schiaparelli's imaginative wit created flamboyant floral
designs. 'Flora' enjoys a pot-pourri of fashion style,
touched by Rococo and Art Deco.

*'Your embroidered garments are
from the earth'*

HENRY KING, 1657

∧ Watercolour and pencil sketches of
flowers in my garden inspire embroidery
designs. The early 19th-century botanical
engraving shown here was the catalyst for
a collection of bags and purses.

Trigynia

Polygynia

Mouse Tail.

In the studio: *creativity*

A rhapsody of colourful blooms takes imagination into a pleasure-ground of pattern. The studio moves outdoors to capture the visual delights of 'Flora': exquisite petal formations, singing colour, fascinating botanical textures with harmonies of foliage and bloom. Gardens are an ever-changing gallery of inspiration and spring palettes fizz with citrus shades while daffodil, narcissus, crocus, primrose and emerging tulips intrigue the eye. June in bloom indulges the senses with fragrant roses, and summer blooms hit vibrant notes in bright palettes of poppies, lilies, marigolds and dazzling dahlias.

Beyond the borders of an embroiderer's garden the *joie de vivre* of wildflower meadows entice creativity into a freer playground of plants. Each unique flower inspires individual designs for decorative stitch.

Paintings and drawings stimulate ideas; the eye selects floral imagery, exploring the interface of inspiration and artistic expression. Pure white watercolour paper is the background for botanical studies. Prior to drawing, surfaces are coated with sweeping washes of subtle colour. Tinting papers achieves a colour resonance, setting the mood before drawing and suggesting colour stories for fabrics and threads. Fabric paints, iridescent acrylics, metallic sheens and interference paints can enhance the paper surface with sponged and brushed textures. Watercolour washes, highlighted by detailed crayon drawings, express the pastel charm of delicate blooms such as rose or clematis.

Dahlias demand a different approach, with the drama of inky-black pastel papers creating a bolder impact for the wild spirit of this showy flower. Vivid splashes of crimson, scarlet, maroon, flame, magenta, orange and yellows plus Schiaparelli's shocking pink create an explosion of colour as flowerheads dance across the paper. Oil pastels and crayons explore dahlia petal textures: raggedy, spiky or velvety. This study directly shaped 'Mexicana' (pages 74–75), where irregular arrangements of flowers, leaves and buds are references for scale, design, colour and embroidered surfaces. Silky rayons interplay with sketches to suggest a palette of embroidery threads.

The dual passion of gardening and botanical painting flows through the 'Flora' collection, enriching the design. Each theme reflects plant personalities through creative stitch and experimental cross-referencing of techniques with fashion shapes. 'Flora' plucks a selection of the bright and the beautiful to radiate across fashion fabrics and accessories. The brilliance of blooms captivates the eye, inspiring a rich diversity for embroidery. Graphic stitches, painterly appliqué, botanical beadwork, textural surfaces, ornate fabric manipulations and stitched laces achieve the translation.

∧ Sketches for 'Mexicana' and 'Dahlia Dance'. Oil pastel and crayon on paper.

In the studio: *interpretations*

Floral paintings and sketches translate with a natural affinity into fabric and thread – flowers and embroidery have a long, historic relationship. Notes and doodles in sketchbooks, in tandem with flower studies, suggest suitable techniques for fabric decoration to style fabrics into fashions and inventive accessories. Design research freely interprets ideas, as spontaneous flower patterns move from paper to fabric, while other designs manoeuvre samples towards final pieces.

The watercolour studies of roses on pages 56 and 69 became an airbrushed, painted confection of silk chiffons and *crêpe de chine* with fabric paints carefully mixed to recreate the delicate rose blushes of the original painting. Roses influence a sequence of fabric manipulations, using different silks, painted chiffons, burgundy organzas and metallic sheers.

Now, let us throw in a wild card of historical reference: *Rosa Gallica* from a 15th-century Book of Hours. Here, interpretation takes another path, with rich metallic machine embroidery and pearl-encrusted details to take the rose to an ornate finish on black quilted silk, ready to ramble across evening wear.

In contrast, 'Botanical Reticules' (pages 62–65) encourages lateral thinking by delving into the world of botany, inspiring a collection of purses. Splashed with spring colour and pewter shades (reference: antique steel engravings), the design is inspired by Jane Austen fashions and 18th-century reticules. Multi-faceted elements conjure bizarre textures for bijoux bags.

Dahlia patterns are given a vibrant Latino interpretation with colourful silk organzas in hot sizzling shades of magenta, ruby, scarlet, plus a twist of lemon and lime. A frenzy of layered appliqué petals (pages 78–79) creates lively decorations to spin across skirts.

The making of fashion fabrics follows an intuitive route, with samples, tested on the figure or a tailor's stand, allowing embellished surfaces to explore and enhance form naturally. Paper and pencil, sketchbook and notebook are as relevant now as in the first *en plein air* botanical studies.

∧ Stitching a machine-embroidered edging for a 'Botanical Reticule'.

< 'Botanical Reticule'. Wired silk organza appliqué, layered and stitched onto a cylindrical fabric form.

'Botanical Reticules'
Samples and sketches

Botanical details suggest starting points
for fabric manipulation. Here, slender
lamé rouleaux, wired, padded and beaded,
intertwine ready to form a filigree purse
shell. Stitched ribbons of metallic organza
loop and twist, suggesting surface textures
or a tassel of trailing tendrils (see Studio
Techniques: Bias ribbons). Dense convoluted
ruffles of wired bias strips cover a cylindrical
pod (see Studio Techniques: Wired ruffles)
and layers of pointed organza petals
surround a cylindrical shape. A gathered
ruche of silk satin creates a sumptuous
surface inspired by a *Scabiosa* flower.

Classical characteristics of flowers, as
illustrated in early botanical drawings and
historic engravings, reveal the complexity of
flora. Each genus of flowers displays unique
features of petals, sepals and stamens. Close
study of plants through painterly sketches
encourages a free analysis of flower forms
and gives direction for colour stories. These
develop naturally through interpretations
of paint and pencil – graphite, silver washes,
chartreuse, lemon and grey-greens. The
imagination shapes pattern and texture,
inspiring fantasy bags and secret reticules.

STUDIO TECHNIQUES:

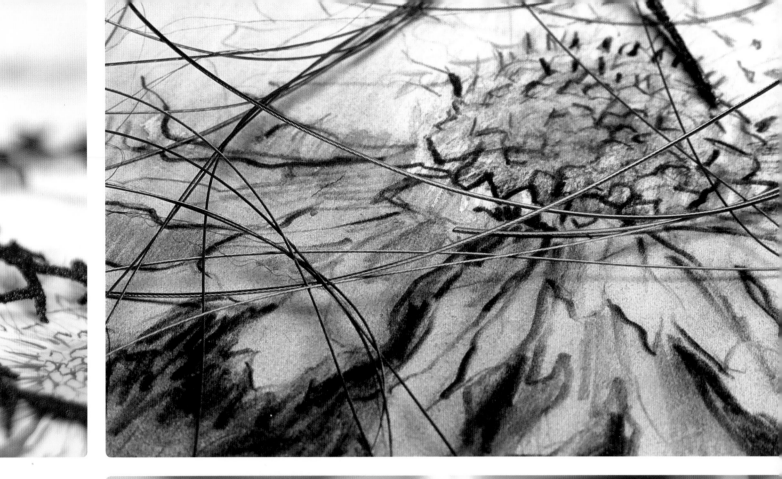

'Botanical Reticules'
Purses

Function and fantasy intertwine, shaping a collection of petite purses. Reticules (from the Latin *reticulum*, a net), dangled from the wrists of the fashionable in the 1800s. These small drawstring purses held the secrets of a society lady's life – love letters, dance cards, rouge! The whimsical elements of the 'reticule' tease embroidery into three-dimensional creations.

Accessory designs extract details of botanical textures to inspire surface manipulation and inventive structures. Colour explores a zestful spring palette of tangerine, lime, primrose and fresh leaf-greens, adding contrast with a steely patina of metallics: silvers and gunmetals. The creation of three-dimensional forms with fabric and stitch evolves through a sequence of design drawings and paper patterns. Botanical reticules analyse the fascinating details of plants with a botanist's eye inspiring an embroiderer's art.

STUDIO TECHNIQUES:

Beadwork	page 82
Machine lace	page 87
Machine-embroidered flowers	page 87
Machine-stitched patterns	page 89

> 'Foliage Fancy'. An eccentric bijou reticule playfully mixes textures – a cylindrical shape encrusted with beads, sequins and chartreuse crystals with a frenzy of machine-stitched tendrils creating a bizarre fringe.

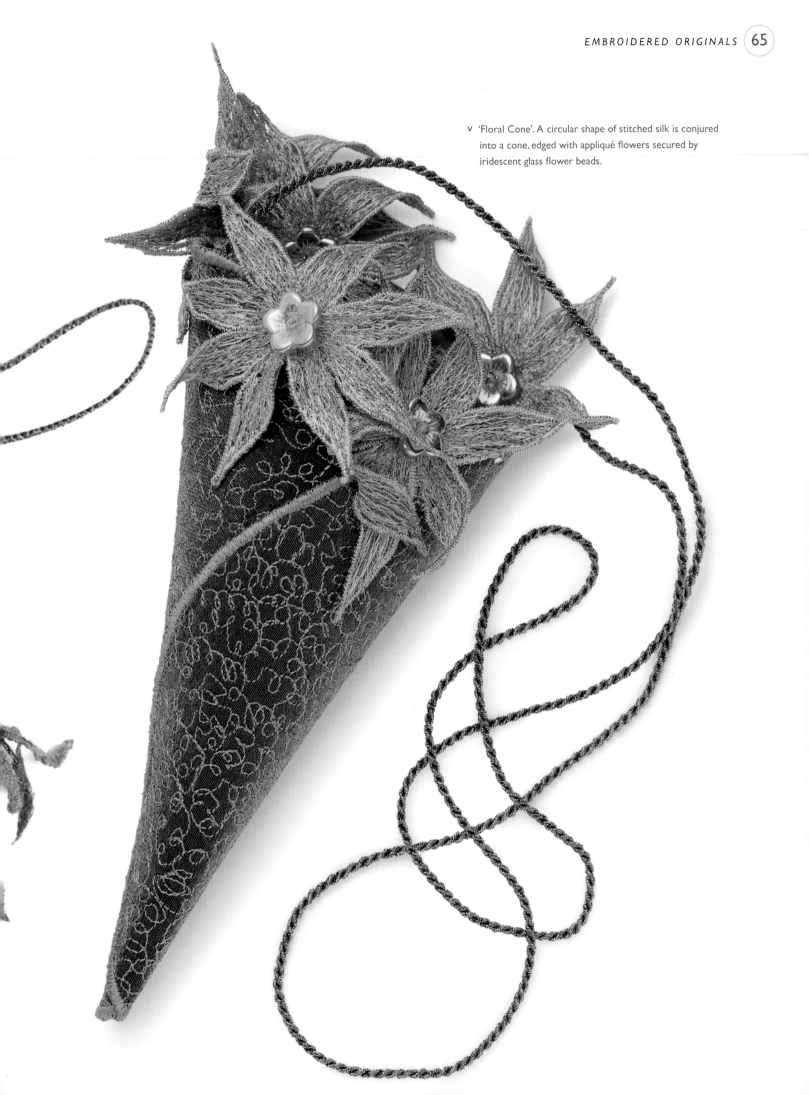

∨ 'Floral Cone'. A circular shape of stitched silk is conjured
into a cone, edged with appliqué flowers secured by
iridescent glass flower beads.

'Rococo'
Fashion samples

The 'Rococo' samples fuse French romance of the 18th century with the beauty of old-fashioned English roses, inspiring surfaces of elaborate embellishment. Fanciful formations of metallic organzas glisten like sugared bonbons and florid textures have all the indulgence of a Marie Antoinette gown.

A confection of ruched blooms, freely created from folded pieces of silk organza, are hand-stitched and gathered to form rose flowers and buds. Three-dimensional petals accent the glints of silver and pale gold organzas, while twists and turns of manipulated metallic sheers create frivolous reliefs, highlighted with lustrous details of freshwater pearls.

Surfaces of hand-stitched organza fragments form a background texture of ruching and beading, which ripples around the roses like fondant icing. Delicate shades of flesh-pinks, shell-pinks, pale *eau-de-nil*, oyster and champagne, all touched with metallic shimmer, enhance the mood of romance.

Fashion details are revealed in portrait paintings of the Rococo period and these provide inspiration. The painters include Jean Honoré Fragonard, François Boucher and the initiator of style, Jean Watteau. In Boucher's painting of Madame de Pompadour, she is adorned head to toe in ruffles, bows, ruched trims – a frothy mélange of manipulation techniques. Historic costumes are a rich resource for embroidery and opulent court dress can be reinvented and refined to create contemporary designs.

The fabrics chosen to interpret this sample cling to the luxury of Rococo's origins but exchanging silks for calicos, muslins and scrims. Using dried-rose shades instead of the tempting sugar candy colours of Marie Antoinette's finery could style a shabby chic.

STUDIO TECHNIQUES:	
Manipulation	page 90
Machine-embroidered flowers	page 87

< Manipulated metallic organza roses for 'Rococo' collection.

∧ In this appliqué detail for a jacket, the petals of 'Rosa Gallica' were recreated with metallic stitchery and pearls and then applied to quilted black silk.

'A Rose is a Rose'
Silk corsages

A passion for roses inspires silk corsages, delicate sheer petals in pastel tints which echo the fragile flora of a watercolour sketch. Since classical times roses have adorned gardens and the varieties that blossom in English gardens during June reflect diverse origins. These embroidered specimens, which ramble a rhythmic trail of shaded rouleaux, convey the varieties of rose flora with petite rosebuds, layered petals of China roses and double damask, climbing tea roses and the famous Bourbon roses of the 18th century.

The free composition of flowers, stems, buds and leaves in the sketches suggests the corsage formation. The roses, deftly expressed in pencil and watercolour crayons, influence a gentle palette of painted silk sheers. Chiffons, *crêpe de chine* and organza are sprayed and shaded with an airbrush, creating pinks and peachy blushes on ivory silks, with hints of lavenders and mauves. Hand-painted golds give sun-kissed shimmer and pearlised glints streak the petals of Rosa Celeste.

Machine stitching, cutwork appliqué, hand ruching, pleating and gathering, together shape each floral corsage. The dainty edges are clipped and beaded and flouncy petals secure centres. Embellishment ideas stem from the intrinsic rose shapes – rosette, cupped, flat, and pointed or pompon. Corsages, a favourite of 19th-century fashions, were used to accent hats, parasols, gowns and coats. Modern fashions continue that love affair with the corsage.

The allure of the rose has always entranced gardeners, artists and embroiderers, using flora elegantly to decorate evening dresses, shape bags, inspire textures, structure hats or trim floaty lingerie. Madame du Barry was so enraptured with roses that she slept in a gilded bed under a canopy of roses. Corsages form fashion accents and decorations for more elaborate wearables or, perhaps, interior textiles in the Versailles style.

STUDIO TECHNIQUES:

'Belle Courtisanne'
Samples for cuffs and armlets

Black, anthracite and rose-pinks offer dramatic contrasts to the pale prettiness of painted corsages. An air of elegance and glamour pervades the studio samples and sketches where a 1950 fashion photograph by Irving Penn is the catalyst for a collection of evening accessories. The model wears a classic black evening gown, accessorised with long black gloves; the *pièce de résistance* is a corsage of three stunning silk roses adorning one glove. Sketches of a beautiful Bourbon rose, the flower opening in a rosette of confused petals, inspires a similar corsage and the thorny branch sparks ideas for a complex embroidered lace pattern. A 1950s dance glove, retrieved from a dressing-up chest, takes design directions into fashion accessories.

Techniques feature machine-stitched *guipure* lace in metallic pewters, anthracite and charcoal, the surfaces studded with sparkling amethyst glass beads and gunmetal sequins. Ruched and gathered powder-pink organza forms a rose, a flourish for a lace armlet. The embroidered lace fabrics are shaped into cuffs and armlets, or suggest designs for an embellished bodice panel.

For the Elizabethans, embroidered gloves were a prized possession and Elsa Schiaparelli's 1930s armlets reflected true style, an accessory to intrigue — and to inspire embroiderers.

STUDIO TECHNIQUES:

Machine lace	page 87
Ruched roses	page 91

'Fleur'
Evening bag

Sensuous silk petals create a flirty embellishment for an evening bag. The rich palette of ruby reds, bronze metallics and gold is evocative of the Art Deco era, as is the simple, semi-circular shape.

The romance of the rose finds new expression in an elegant form as a functional accessory. A free flourish of silk organza petals contrasts with the geometric precision of quilted gold metallic organza layered over crimson silk. Floral appliqué accents carefully conceal the tied closure of the bag top. Design, decoration and construction are in complete harmony, evolving through sketches, paper patterns and samples. Creative stitch explores three-dimensional forms, enhancing an evening bag with texture and lavish gestures of floral appliqué, enriched with freshwater pearls and sequins.

Fine-crafted details give a unique hallmark to 'Fleur', reminiscent of the fabulous embroideries of the Paris ateliers in the 1920s. The genius of Erté and Paul Poiret inspired extravagant, innovative fashions with ornate stitched surfaces. The brilliance of the Jazz Age is also reflected in the textiles of Atelier Martine, Maison Lallement and Les Callot Soeurs, who produced exquisite hand and machine embroideries. These artistic works remain a splendid resource for study.

For centuries, embroidered bags have been an object of desire – an accessory that continues to intrigue, amuse and inspire the creative touch of textile artists.

STUDIO TECHNIQUES:

Quilting	page 92
Appliqué sheers	page 81
Beadwork	page 82

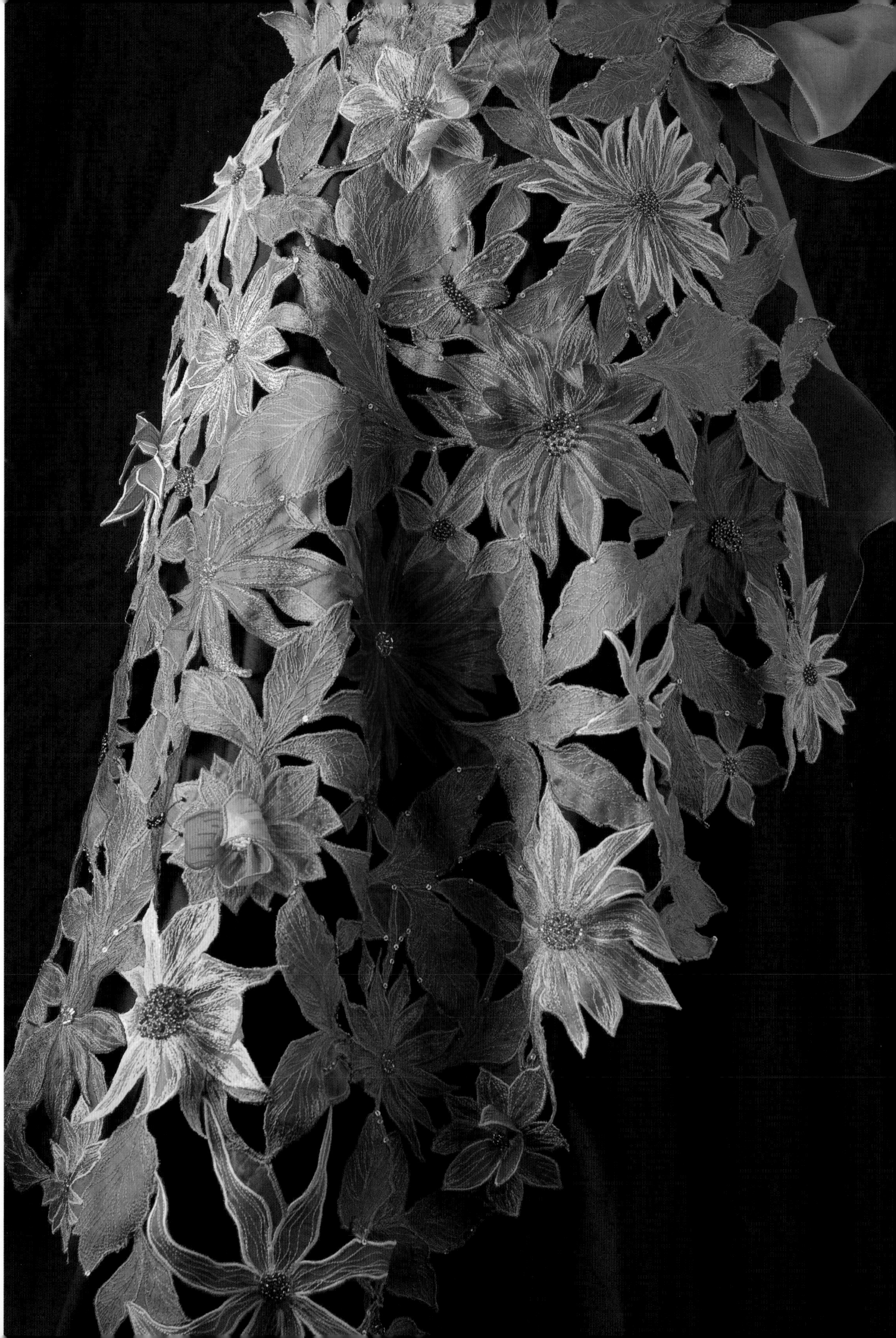

'Mexicana'
Embroidered cut-out lace skirt

Dazzling dahlia heads explode in starbursts of colour on inky-black papers. These showy flowers spin energetically with Latino rhythm, striking lively designs for embroidery. A Mexican mix of bright colours includes hot pinks, magenta, flame red, yellow, lime, scarlet, mauve and cactus greens, all stitched, appliquéd and beaded – a 'flower-power' paradise to adorn the body. The flamboyant nature of 'Mexicana' references the dahlia's origins with Mexican gardens and traditional costumes – a Latin tempo influences design and style. The asymmetric 'apron-skirt', sashed at the waistline and slashed at the sides, is layered over black silk to accentuate cutwork appliqué, adding drama to the zingy colours. In the spirit of dance music, the embellished fabric can change into a split tango skirt, worn with black stockings.

Stitch changes the nature of fabrics, and free machine embroidery influences the drape and flow of materials. The garment shape evolved from a single stitched dahlia on a length of silk organza. Machine-embroidered cutwork experiments grew, flower by flower, leaf by leaf, to evolve as a skirt, embellished with over thirty blooms. Fabrics and threads define the character of the fashion fabric: green silk organza plays a background role with multicolour silks forming flower appliqué. Viscose threads add soft lustre to embroidered petals and leaves, while satin-stitch edgings define the precise shapes. Meticulous cutwork creates movement and drape, giving dahlias the freedom to dance across the silk.

Like the tulip mania of the 1600s, dahlias sparked passions in the 19th century, rising to star status with florists and gardeners. A flower to inspire and enhance fashion, each unique variety suggests striking textures for appliqué. Consider the shapes of pompon, anemone, collerette, cactus and waterlily dahlias. The vibrant flora dazzles the senses with stitched splendour.

STUDIO TECHNIQUES:

Embroidered flamboyance	page 85
Appliqué sheers	page 81
Machine-embroidered flowers	page 87

∨ These dahlia corsages were made from silk organza appliqué petals, manipulated and beaded.

∨ This sketch of dahlias inspired a vibrant palette of threads for the 'Mexicana' skirt shown on page 74.

'Dahlia Dance'
Appliqué organza skirt

A swirling sheer skirt gives dahlia flowers a final flounce with splashes of vivid colour to catch the eye, as a swish of petals falls towards the hemline. In contrast to the stitch frenzy of 'Mexicana', this skirt takes a trio of dahlias into appliqué.

Images of 1950s dance dresses, with their voluminous layers of tulle petticoats clinched at the waist with belts or sashes, inspire a simple flared, circular ankle-length skirt. A bias ribbon of citrus green runs around the hemline, defining the rhythmic sway of inky silk organza, and a wide floaty sash shapes the waistline. Retro-chic influences style, and sketches of dwarf dahlias extract the essence of colour and texture for embroidery.

The fancy structures of dahlia heads – the quilled florets, tubular, serrated, double-layered, spiky cactus – are dream textures for artful needles to ruche, gather and ruffle.

Shocking-pink petals are applied to the underside of the organza to create a shadow shape of hazy purple set against the flourish of petals on the top surface which sing out with their true colours. Fussy flower centres are ruched and gathered, rising from flat appliqué petals enhanced with beads and sequin sparkle.

The Mexican dahlia, extrovert and super-showy, offers fashion an exciting array of decorative approaches.

STUDIO TECHNIQUES:

Appliqué sheers	page 81
Gathered surfaces	page 86

CHAPTER 4

STUDIO TECHNIQUES

Airbrushed fabrics

Airbrush techniques of spray painting give a variety of effects on fabric. Try free-spraying backgrounds, spraying over stencils, forming abstract pattern layers with template masks, spraying precise areas of colour, or making splatter textures.

Use basic airbrush equipment such as the Badger Hobby model (with wide nozzle, simple air valve control and screw-fit jars) and an electric compressor (or cans of compressed air). Fabric paints, used on the textiles illustrated, are helizarin pigments mixed with a binder (screen-printing) diluted ready for spraying. The leaves design (below) uses several shades of green, sprayed on cream medium-weight habutai silk.

AIRBRUSHED APPLIQUÉ LEAVES

Freehand spraying, without stencils or masks, is perfect for creating subtle variations of colour over a larger area of fabric.

Stretching material over a surface (such as a padded print table) avoids wrinkles when the material gets wet from spraying.

For leaves, the silk was freely sprayed and dried. Next, Bondaweb (fusible webbing) was fused to the wrong side of the silk and leaf shapes drawn on the paper backing. Leaves were cut out, the paper removed and then placed gum side onto organza. Iron to bond, using baking parchment between iron and organza.

Angelina fibres

These soft, shimmering polyester fibres offer exciting applications for creative textiles. The 'Hot Fix' fibres fuse together, forming sparkly webs; 'Standard' or 'Metallic' fibres intermix and fuse – add a little 'Hot Fix' for a variety of metallic effects.

Angelina can create a complete fabric – see the 'Vita Alba' fichu (page 20), where embellishments integrate Angelina with machine-embroidered lace techniques.

For this piece a fused mesh of iridescence was formed by spreading fibres loosely between sheets of baking parchment, and ironing. This produced a gossamer mesh, ready for free machining in Supertwist opal-colour no.30 to give texture and stability to the fragile surface. Sequins were then hand stitched.

Angelina fibres (continued)

ANGELINA LAYERED FABRIC

The shimmering material of the 'Away with the Fairies' cape (page 2) combined the processes described opposite.

Coloured silk snippets in matching butterfly shades were fused between the layers of bluish-gold Angelina fibres. Large areas of fused material were made and machine stitched with Madeira FS gold, onto a background of silk organza. The panels were then seamed and stitched sequins added, securing any loose silk. Angelina was used here with machine embroidery, with water-soluble film to stabilise, to create appliqué butterflies.

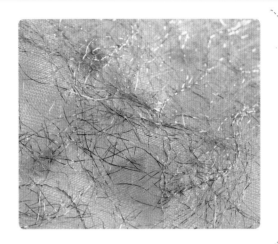

Appliqué sheers

BONDED FERN LEAVES

Appliqué requires a delicate technique for sheers. Rayon no.40 machine thread (with a size 75 machine needle) was used for the stitching. Using the airbrushed silk pieces, the method is as described for 'Airbrushed appliqué leaves', left: fusing, creating shapes, cutting out and fusing again. The weight of the appliqué silk is important – if it is too fine, the Bondaweb gum will be visible on the right side.

Simple bonding suits the complex, pinnate fern leaf. It requires no precise edging stitch as the close grain of the silk and the fusible coating will prevent fraying. Free machine embroidery dances over the silk leaf and textured stitch patterns secure the leaf appliqué.

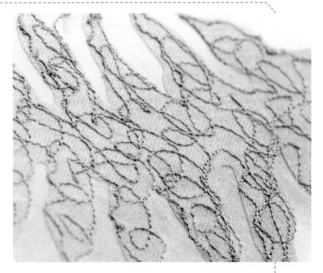

FLAT AND RELIEF DAHLIA PETALS

Contrasting with simple bonded appliqué, the manipulated petal layers were formed from plain organza, attached to a shot silk organza. The flower shape can be created in four ways.

1 Place a square of magenta organza under the organza background and stitch petal shapes from the right side, using paper templates. Straight stitch the outline, remove the paper and then stitch close zigzag (satin stitch) over the straight stitch. Clip away the excess magenta organza, revealing petals in muted shades (shadow appliqué).
2 Use the same method as 1 but apply magenta organza to the top surface.
3 Relief petals are made in a frame (unlike the above appliqué) but using the same method: straight stitch with precise satin edging. These are then cut out.
4 The petals are attached with hand stitching to the flat appliqué petals and sequins hand stitched to the ends of the petals.

Appliqué sheers (continued)

LEAF APPLIQUÉ EDGING

This method was used to create decorative edgings with appliqué stitching (page 81) where free machine embroidery (darning foot / feed-dog lowered) and a finishing edge stitch of close zigzag/satin stitch (appliqué foot / feed-dog up) were worked in an embroidery frame.

At the leaf tips, the satin stitch was tapered to avoid a bulky finish. In this sample, the organza was a single thickness (double layers of sheers will give stiffer relief appliqué). Over 50 leaves, in different sizes, were made for this stole edging. Here, fine smooth gold machine thread (no.50) gave a firmer edge. Tiny sequins were hand stitched.

WIRED EDGINGS

Method as above. Leafy layers were made using a combination of double and single thicknesses of organza for a semi-transparent look. Fine brass wire, 28 or 34 gauge, was used with an embroidery or couching foot, passing the wire through a hole in the foot.

The wire was trapped and covered by satin stitch, which allowed careful manipulation at the leaf tips. The wire ends were concealed at the leaf bases and hand stitched to the reticule structure. Sequins were hand stitched.

Beadwork

Beads add dimension to surface decoration, creating sparkles, encrusted dazzle, enriching colour and iridescence.

Beads of all shapes, sizes and materials enhance fashion fabrics as finishing details, or give textural focus. Hand beading was used for embroideries, not tambour beading, where fabric is framed. Sequins can also be attached by machine. Beads for embellishment are rich and diverse:

- Japanese and Czech glass seed and bugle beads
- Czech pressed glass shapes – teardrops, hearts, petals etc. – in opalescent finishes
- Swarovski crystals, semi-precious stones, e.g. quartz, aquamarine
- Japanese freshwater and cultured pearls.

The internet is a rich source for all types of bead suppliers. Try using your favourite search engine to locate different products.

Beadwork (continued)

FLOWER CENTRES

Beadwork encrusts a flower and raised bead textures contrast with fragile Angelina surfaces.

Here, imitation pearls and Czech glass beads were stitched with transparent Nymo thread, using a millinery (straw) needle no.10, or a beading needle. To attach beads, use double back stitch on the reverse, passing the needle to the right side of the fabric through the glass bead, then the pearl. Return down the centre of the glass bead, taking the needle to the reverse – the pearl sits on top of the glass bead. (Slight tension, when returning the needle to the back, secures the position of the pearl.) For single beads, bring the needle to the front and pick up the bead. Return to the back of the fabric and back stitch, then bring the needle to the front for the next bead. Dense beadwork changes the weight and drape of fabrics.

RANDOM TEXTURES

Hand beadwork, freely scattered on the surface, contrasts with the precision of the flower centres or with the delicate beaded edges of sheer roses. When creating random textures, be guided by the selected design theme and the chosen fabrics. Planning arrangements of bead patterns can follow an intuitive direction. Prior to stitching, place beads on the fabric surface to help select texture, colour and scale. Observe design sources for pattern and composition ideas.

The sample, right, explores iridescence on a dark palette. The spiky, frosted foiled silk is enhanced with an extra twinkle from iridescent, cupped sequins and the embossed lustre of pearls and glass beads. Here the beadwork randomly dances across the 'Night Frost' bodice.

Other approaches for random textures:
- Thread a length of thread with different beads, then couch onto a firm base in rhythmic trails.
- Paint metallic surfaces, gather, manipulate and then bead the irregular cavities.
- Create dense areas of beadwork, using a 'pick & mix' of bugles, seed and glass shapes.
- Dazzle the surface with sequin shimmer, mixing cup and flat sequins in a variety of sizes.
- Nestle tiny beads or pearls in the undulations of free machine quilting.

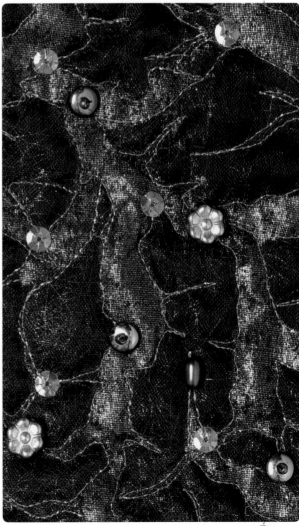

To attach the beads, use a variety of threads: strong beading Nymo for firm textures, lengths and droplets, metallic machine thread for delicate sequins. Also consider polyester thread or waxed threads.

Beadwork (continued)

BEADED CORDS

Machine-wrapped cords were made by stitching close zigzag stitches over fine cord. This stitching was repeated two or three times to ensure that the cord was well covered.

Hand-stitched seed beads were added by gliding a millinery needle (size 10) through the zigzag and beads secured at intervals. For droplets on the cord end, a double thread was used, passing the needle through the drop. Pick up the seed bead, return the needle back through the drop and into the cord to end.

BEADED EDGINGS – AIRBRUSHED ROSE

Iridescent glass seed beads flicker around an organza flower.

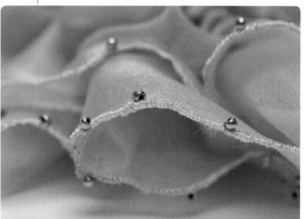

A beading needle (size 12), threaded with the same iridescent thread as the satin stitch edge, glides under the stitches attaching beads randomly. These delicate details contrast with the encrusted centre of freshwater pearls.

Sequins can be stitched on leaf edges – make two stitches to anchor the sequin (see Leaf Appliqué page 82).

Variations of beaded edges can be seen throughout the book.

Chain stitch – vintage stitches

Chain stitch creates rhythmic patterns of intertwining lines of linked loops to enhance a sheer silk.

Here, the glade-green organza is streaked with metallic colours, using Markal (Shiva) sticks, before stitching. The chain stitch is worked in Madeira FS gold thread, creating a slightly textured surface; finer threads can also be used. An antique sewing-machine, such as a Willcox & Gibbs, offers another decorative stitch for embroidery. Worked with a single thread (top spool only) and a rotating hook mechanism, a chain stitch is created on the underside of the fabric with a straight stitch on the upper side.

To achieve the free-moving pattern of lines, the fabric is manipulated under the needle and gently coaxed to the right and left in curving movements. The Cornelli machine produces a similar chain stitch.

This fabric was later manipulated and beaded for the 'Glade' collection of samples (see page 49).

Cut-out lace

WHITE SHEERS

The 'Drift' fabrics in Chapter 1 explore decorative stitch, white on white. Cut-out organzas push the boundaries of machine cut-out lace, playing with larger-scale cut-away areas. Traditional processes, such as textiles produced using the Swiss Schiffli machine, were reinvented using a domestic Bernina sewing machine. The design of wavy lines was marked on white silk organza, using a self-erasing marker. These wavy lines were drawn across the bias grain and straight stitch was used to follow the marker lines. Close zigzag stitch covers the straight stitch giving a delicate edge for cutting. The naturally firm silk required no hoop for machine stitching. It was then carefully trimmed by hand and the zigzag edge beaded. The bias cut-outs created a fluid drape in the silk.

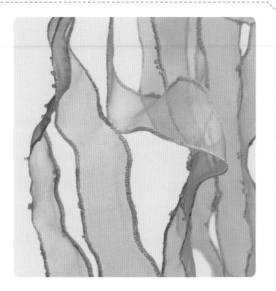

EMBROIDERED FLAMBOYANCE

The 'Mexicana' skirt (pages 74–75) features a mix of embroidery techniques: appliqué, relief appliqué, shadow appliqué, free machine embroidery, cutwork and hand beading. As an elaborate cut-out lace, embroidery was used to shape a fabric in stages and layers. One metre of shot green silk organza formed the base appliqué fabric, then layers of coloured silk pieces (chiffon, organza, habutai silk) create petal layers and leaves. Machine embroidery was used to pattern each motif and a variable satin stitch enclosed each shape. The buds, petals, leaves and stems form interlocking networks of edged shapes. Curved appliqué scissors were used to trim away the background fabric. Rayon machine threads (nos 30 and 40) give a soft drape to the fabric.

Decorative edging – ruffled flounce

This technique is good for decorative edgings – see 'Night Frost' on pages 26–27. Here, a ruffled organza flounce was edged with satin stitch in an iridescent thread. The satin stitch edge was worked at least ½in./12mm from the raw edge of the fabric as this excess material prevents the edge from puckering under the presser foot. Slight tension with the hands also prevents sheer fabric from gathering under the foot during stitching.

Synthetic fabrics require more control. Trim away excess fabric from satin stitch after stitching. For a bolder effect, a second row of stitching can be worked directly over the first trimmed satin stitch edge – a firmer tension with the hands is needed here, and a slight increase in stitch length.

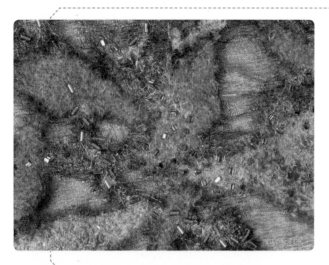

Embellisher

The embellisher machine can be used to create soft, velvety, plush textures on black silk organza. Heavier fabrics are the usual choice for needle felting with the embellisher but this sample reveals the potential for sheers. Black silk organza, medium weight, was used as a double layer, with a filling of shapes cut from olive-green dupion. The embellisher meshed the three fabrics together, texturing the olive-green silk into the organza layers and resulting in a surface pile of mossy shades.

Random puckering shadowed the textures, creating an inventive fashion fabric. Glass bugle beads enhanced the surface pattern.

Foiled silks

Foiling adds metallic lustre to silk with rich effects, similar to gold/silver leaf. This gives diverse applications for decorating a range of fabrics, before stitch.

In 'Night Frost' (pages 26–27) it creates iridescence on black silk, with glints of abstract foiled textures fused with Bondaweb. The final design for the 'Night Frost' bodice refines foiling by fusing spiky cut-outs of Bondaweb to silk (iron between non-stick paper) and foiling the revealed gum shapes.

Layering sheers over foils reduces glitter and protects the metallic coatings. The bodice panel was layered with black silk organza before quilting.

Gathered surfaces

Gathering and furrowing are manipulation techniques for fabrics. 'Botanical Reticule' (page 62) illustrates a circular texture of gathered, furrowed silk satin with beadwork details.

Manipulation can create rich surfaces for accessories or accents for garments such as shawl collars. Fabric for gathering should be twice the size of the final area.

The purse shown has a circular base of bonded Vilene. Silk was gathered and stitched to the outer edge of the base, the puffy shape gradually reducing with stitch. The rearranged furrows were stitched to the base until the gathered texture was finished. Finally, beads were added.

Fabrics can be painted prior to gathering. See also Painted fabrics (page 91) and the gathered flower centres on pages 68–69.

Machine-embroidered flowers

Individual floral motifs were made by framing sheer fabric in an embroidery hoop and then using free machine stitching with the feed-dog down and a darning foot attached.

Rayon threads were used for the sample illustrated. Using straight stitch (the linear patterns), gradually build the colours as the needle moves into the centre and back to the petal edges. As a crayon creates marks on paper, the machine needle draws with lines of thread. The outer edge of the flower can be edged with narrow satin stitch using either an appliqué foot and teeth up or, for a less uniform satin stitch, a darning foot with the feed-dog down. Cut away excess fabric after machining the edge.

Machine lace

FROSTED

Machine embroidery, or *guipure** lace, creates an openwork fabric out of thread. Worked on firm water-soluble film, which supports free machining without a hoop, the needle stitches a fine mesh, within a V-shape – see 'Frost', pages 16–17. Opalescent threads in three shades (Supertwist Opal no.30) create a complex organic pattern of criss-crossing lines. For a fine mesh, work one or two rows of straight stitch; four to six rows form broader lines. The water-soluble film is manipulated in different directions during free machining (darning foot / feed-dog down), creating rhythmic patterns across the V-shape. Satin stitch (embroidery foot / feed-dog up) covers the core lines, with varied stitch width. Change the thread shades and the stitch textures – try narrow lines contrasting with thicker, corded lines to give a natural look. Trim the excess film, immerse in cold water, and rinse repeatedly. Pin to shape and dry naturally.

* Chemical or burnt-out lace imitating handmade lace, e.g. Venetian

FROST FLOWER

Here, a single lace motif was worked in a hoop, using a light water-soluble stabiliser on sheer fabric.

The petal shapes were drawn on the film with a Magic Marker. Petal shapes were outlined 2–3 times with straight stitch. For the mesh filling, single lines criss-cross the petal to touch the outline. Satin stitch was used on the petal outline, tapering at points.

The centres of the flower petals were manipulated into shape before hand beading.

Machine lace (continued)

VIRIDIS LACE 1

The thread used makes a tremendous difference. For this piece, worked as before, silky rayon (100% viscose) machine threads created a machine lace with a soft weight and drape. Lace structures made only of metallic threads created a firmer surface. Metallic threads (30 and 50) blended with rayon, give sparkle on 'Viridis' lace. Threads, like paints, can blend to create gradations of greens and textural mixes. Altering bobbin tensions, or the top thread, gives subtle changes of colour and texture; metallic in the bobbin creates flickers of surface sparkle.

VIRIDIS LACE 2

Free machine embroidery can translate spring foliage into stitch. Hot-water-soluble fabric, a white voile-like material, 44in./111cm wide, makes a good support for free embroidery and attaching appliqué or bonded shapes. It is also useful for drawing the design, using a hard pencil.

Use a hoop for stitching, drop the feed-dog and use a darning foot. Here, the foliage shapes were drawn on water-soluble fabric, ready to stitch. Patterns, as described below, filled the leaves and plant shapes, while interlocking straight stitches created criss-cross meshes, scribble doodles and so on. A lace structure grew freely without an exact pre-planned design. The embroidery was immersed in hot water to dissolve the water-soluble fabric. The lace fabric was pinned to shape, drying naturally. The photo (left) shows work in progress on the voile.

EDGING FOR RETICULE

A metallic thread formed a stiff, densely stitched edging for a reticule on a thick film of cold-water-soluble fabric.

Worked in a frame to aid the free stitching of the decorative pattern (see photo), the thicker no. 20 thread defined precise botanical details. Repeat straight stitch was used initially and was then overstitched with zigzag stitch twice.

FASHION DETAIL

This variation of the previous edging, worked in gunmetal Madeira FS threads (bobbin) and a rayon no.30 thread (top), is stitched less densely with no zigzag (satin stitch).

The lace has the look of Victorian cut-steel jewellery with a pliant texture of openwork embroidery.

Machine-stitch patterns

SCRIBBLE STITCH

For this piece, straight stitch free machine stitching (darning foot / feed-dog dropped) was used over two layers of firm silk organza, with no frame. Linear stitches in rayon no.30 were criss-crossed in open, irregular structures. The material is always cut wider than the finished piece. Hand-hold the fabric firmly with a slight tension, not getting too close to the needle area. Pure silk organza gives a firm, more manageable surface for this technique as synthetics can pucker or slide unless framed in a hoop. Test the tension and stitch length before committing to the fabric. The design was freely sketched on paper prior to stitch, then spontaneously machined to reproduce the design. Scribble stitch can be developed in many ways by over-laying shades, using variegated threads, tighter textures etc.

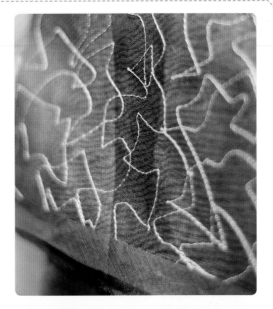

MEANDER AND DOODLE STITCH

Continuous trails of loopy lines were freely stitched on fabric, without a pre-drawn pattern, setting the machine up as for scribble stitch. Free machining spontaneously covered the fabric with a lively doodle of stitches in rayon thread (Madeira Sticku no.30). No frame was used for this sample, as the background of bonded silks gave a stable surface for the free machine stitching. Skilful manipulation under the needle, and gentle pedal action, created a meandering line of loopy patterns which moved across the material. The fabric was then cut into a circle and styled into a cone-shaped reticule (page 65). Similar stitch patterns can be seen on Bonded Fern Leaves (page 81) and in Chapter 2 (pages 32 and 35). For a more controlled meander stitch, see the example in Quilting, free machine (page 92).

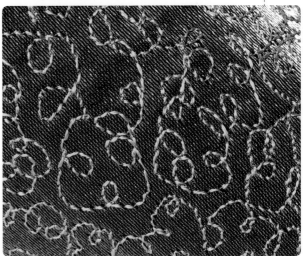

SATIN STITCH MEANDER

Rhythmic lines of satin stitch create flowing surfaces.

Set the machine with the feed-dog teeth up and use the appliqué foot. Stitch in a controlled way to avoid gaps in the satin stitch.

Holding the sides of the fabric, gentle movements were made to the left and right to create swaying patterns of satin stitch. The size of the satin stitch was controlled by manually altering the stitch width, to give tapered lines and wider satin stitch widths. The stitch length was kept an even length of approximately 0.5. Test patterns of stitch length and width on calico before commencing.

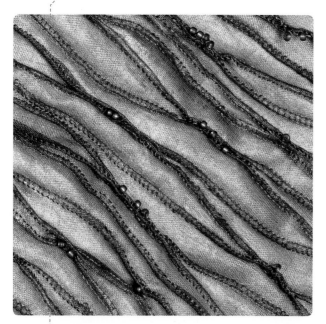

Machine-stitch textures – twin-needled ridges

Twin-needle work can be both functional and decorative, as shown. Here painted silk organza was stitched with rayon thread on top and a fine polyester thread in the bobbin. The top threads create parallel lines of stitch, while the bobbin thread creates an open zigzag stitch. Twin-needles come in different sizes (from 70 to 100) and various widths, to give fine ridges on fine fabrics and broader widths for velvets and calicos.

For metallic threads an embroidery twin-needle was used, which avoids threads fraying. Testing stitch widths for twin-needles prior to stitching can help to avoid breaking the needle on the presser foot. Take care with threading; take threads either side of the tension disc to avoid thread tangle. This sample in straight stitch meanders diagonally across the grain of the sheer. It was then manipulated into free smocked structures to give delicate bark-like cavities.

BIAS RIBBONS

Here, bias strips are made from sheer silk metallic organza. Cut strips (1¼in./32mm wide) in metre lengths. Fold and straight stitch a wavy line the length of the strip, working 3/8in./10mm from fold edge at the widest wave point, to give a gradually undulating line. Satin stitch over the straight stitch line, using a presser foot with feed-dogs up. Keep a slight tension to avoid the strip bunching. Trim away excess fabric from raw edges. The bias ribbons can be manipulated in a various ways: undulating relief loops could be stitched to background fabrics with beads. They could form layered fringes of wavy bias lengths in gradations of colours, or add fancy details to corsages with trailing tendrils of stitched ribbons.

Manipulation
RELIEF ORGANZA RIPPLE

A variation of a flounce, without the flare – not quite a ruche as there is no gathering. Heavy-weight silk organza was cut as broad bias strips (3in./7.5cm before stitch and trim). This was stitched with straight stitch machined ½in./12 mm away from the raw edge (both sides). This line defines the position of the satin stitch. Using silver Supertwist 30 thread (bobbin and top), a normal presser foot and a metallic needle 80, work with the feed-dog up in satin stitch (length 0.5, width 3–3.5). Test the widths before you start. The design contrasts sheer translucence with the precision-stitched silver edge. Close satin stitch on sheers needs to be coaxed through the machine. Trim away excess fabric close to stitches and work rhythmic rippled hand stitching on the lower edge.

Manipulation (continued)

RUCHED ROSES

A fashion sample ('Rococo' pages 66–67) shows hand-manipulated fabric, hand stitched and beaded. Created in metallic silk organza, strips of folded bias and folded straight grain were cut in random lengths (from 18in./45cm to 6in./15.2cm) and varying widths (from 3in./7.5cm to 1in./2.5cm) in double fabric to form relief roses.

The folded lengths were manipulated, twisted into spirals and gathered, just in from the base edges. They were then hand stitched, using a millinery (straw) needle, piercing with the needle through all the twists and gathers at the flower base. You could try ruched textures, a mix of shades in the twists, creating tight coils, open gathers, beaded centres. These could be set in groups or used solo. In the sample shown, the raw edges of the rose bases were stitched to a textured silk ground. A surface of metallic organza fragments created a background where silk pieces, raw edged, were manipulated, and beaded onto silk (bonded to calico).

WIRED RUFFLE

This texture was inspired by a rosette of petals. The samples for 'Botanical Reticules' (pages 64–65) show experiments with manipulation and explore inventive surfaces for 3D shapes. Bias strips (cut 2½in./64mm wide) start the ruffle; fold them in half lengthways, and straight stitch close to the fold edge. Then satin stitch (length 0.5, width 2–3) over the fold edge, trapping fine wire under the satin stitches. Hold the wire with your fingers while stitching or thread through a special foot – some machines have one with a fine hole for wire. Wired bias strips can then be manipulated into ruffles, placed close together so the raw edges are concealed by meandering rows of wired ruffles.

Painted fabrics

Hand-painted fabrics feature in many of the embroidered textiles in the book and iridescent metallic fabric paints (straight from the pots and not diluted) have been used for many effects. For example, in the 'Glade' piece, the texture of gathered, painted organza was created by painting with a wide brush, making quick marks across the fabric. Some fabric paints have an acrylic body and, used lightly, the fabric is still soft; heavier usage of acrylic paints stiffens surfaces. Sponges can also create interesting textures – on damp fabric the paints will merge softly into the fibres but, for more texture, the paints could be worked on dry fabrics. Splatter textures could be made by using diluted paints with a broad paintbrush, flicking the surface with the paint.

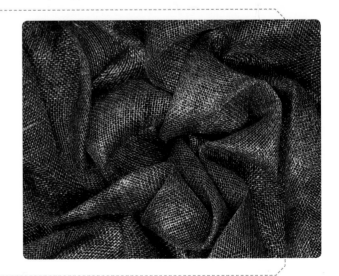

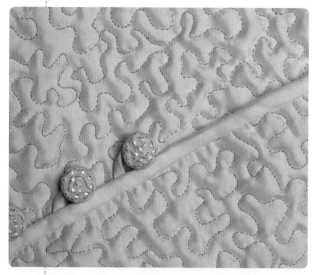

Quilting

FREE MACHINE

Fine gold stitching on ivory silk created this rich surface. With a darning foot and free machine stitching, coax the fabric through the machine, moving gently for curvy lines. The improvised meanders of stitchery should not cross but should flow across the silk in gentle undulations. Variations: close/dense stitched patterns for filling shapes or more open wavy lines to drift over larger-scale quilted areas of fabric. Here, a sandwich of lightweight silk, polyester wadding (2oz) and fine muslin was used. For a lighter, more supple effect, quilt without the backing muslin. This texture is perfect for jackets, coats, waistcoats and interior textiles. Note: Free machine meander stitch can be used on sheers and bonded surfaces (see page 89, Machine-stitch patterns)

GEOMETRIC

Angular precision or exact parallel lines of quilting require a presser foot attachment, to guide line spacing. This is generally an arm which is inserted into the presser foot. A screw can alter the position of the metal arm in relation to the space between the first stitched line and the following ones. The geometric diamonds were created by marking and stitching a diagonal line through all layers and then, with the arm attached, the first stitch line was traced while the next stitch row was formed. One set of parallel lines was created. Then diagonal dissecting lines, which form the diamond pattern, were stitched using the spacer technique. Care is needed to keep the fabric layers smooth to avoid puckers of excess fabric between the lines.

Rouleaux

Basics: Always cut from the bias grain of fabric, which runs diagonally across the straight grain of the fabric, at a 45 degree angle. The straight grain is parallel to the selvedge edge. Cut strips with scissors or a rotary cutter; widths can vary according to fabric and function. The strips for the rouleaux here are cut 1 3/8 in./3.5cm wide.

Stitching: Fold the rouleau strip in half, right sides together, and machine with a polyester thread and a short stitch length. Machine with presser foot down, approximately 5/16in./1cm from the fold (for fabrics that fray, stitch a second row). The tubes can then be turned with a bodkin (leave the ends of the machine threads to thread through the needle) or use a rouleau turner. Tubes can be threaded with a fine-gauge craft wire and quilting wool, and finished with a bead.

Rouleaux (continued)

AIRBRUSHED ROULEAUX
Basics, as above.

For the airbrushed effect, apply paint to silk before stitching the tubes. For example, silk *crêpe de chine* could be airbrushed with fabric paint before the bias strips are cut.

Layers of pastel shades subtly change across the bias length, echoing the tints of rose corsages. Lengths are machined and turned (as before) and padded with one or two strands of quilting wool. Soft padded tubes can be stitched in loops and twists, attached to the underside of flowers. Padded rouleaux can form decorative fastenings: plaited belts, tendrils for fabric jewellery, straps for bags or ornate lacy *décolleté* decorations.

The rouleaux can be enriched with beads and sequins.

HEDERA LACE
Basics, as above.

Gunmetal metallic fabric was chosen here to make the rouleaux – an openwork lace structure. The technique was exploited to produce a lace fabric.

Using both the right and wrong sides of the fabric for the rouleaux tubes results in two subtle shades of gunmetal: a steely grey and a darker anthracite grey/black shade. Unpadded rouleaux were manipulated by hand into stylised plant stems, randomly looping into patterns, pinned, then hand-sewn. Acid-green sequins were hand-stitched to the rouleaux lace at strategic points.

The lace was created to fit the shape of the garment pattern, developing the design on a dressmaker's dummy stand.

ROULEAUX LOOPS AS A DECORATIVE EDGING
Functional fastenings can inspire fashion trims.

Here, the usual single loops, spaced for buttons, have been replaced by a line of repeated loops which give a fringe effect. The rouleaux were placed behind a bias-bound edge. A rouleau length of 50–60in./127–152cm makes about twenty five loops. The sample shown used a 30in./76.2cm trim length.

The rouleaux were made of metallic silk dupion. Try this with variable lengths, colour changes, a mix of fine and thicker tubes, beaded ends, knotted ends or frayed ends.

About the author

A fascination for vintage clothes and antique embroideries has always been with me and this, together with the countryside environment of my 1950s childhood on a farm, sowed the seeds for the continuing love affair with nature which inspired this book.

Flowers hold a special magic for me and their transient beauty has nurtured numerous creations, from the English flora which entranced the Elizabethan age to the exotic water lily that caught the eye of fashion designer Bill Gibb in 1976. My embroidery took to the couture catwalk, attracting commissions for bespoke bridal and evening wear.

Research is a vital facet of the design process and it touches the mood of many themes. Fabrics of the past have influenced key stages in my embroidered works, tilting concepts into new directions.

Nature and nostalgia continue to infuse the language of my embroidery, with romance and fantasy styling a fashion pzazz.

SUE RANGELEY

∧ Dahlia corsage in shot silk organza with machine appliqué.

∧ Details of machine-embroidered edging for a purse from the 'Botanical Reticules' collection.

Costume collections are a wonderful resource for understanding fashion shapes and studying the details of embroidery techniques, and couture craft processes. These can be reinvented in amazing ways. A glimpse of embroidered stomachers in the Victoria & Albert Museum started the journey for the 'Frost' stitched laces shown on pages 16–19.

These are a total contrast to the embroidered jackets of Elsa Schiaparelli. A precious sketchbook of those exquisite pieces still brings a tingle of delight and memories of a visit to the Metropolitan Museum of Art in New York. There I sat in a study room, surrounded by her creations. My early 1980s work – quilted, embroidered boleros in rich metallic stitchery – pay homage to that fabulous designer's work.

The Oxfordshire landscape has been the backdrop to my studio for nearly thirty years; my home, in a small Cotswold town, is the setting for my creative space. The immediate vista of my flower garden nurtures my creative dreams, which can be seen throughout the book. Designs can emerge naturally from the garden via sketches and paintings or, less romantically, while tidying a tangle of undergrowth.

An American visitor once remarked that my studio, with its romantic bric-à-brac, reminded her of Lara's home in the film *Dr Zhivago*. Pasternak, in one of the 'Zhivago' poems to Olga Ivinskaya, role model for Lara, writes: 'At one o'clock we shall sit down to table. At three we shall rise, I with my book, you with your embroidery.'

< 'Night Flight'. Evening cape.
Glorious gold highlights a flight of moths in a scintillating
array of metallic textures. Deep purple velvet creates a
dramatic contrast for the embellished insects which scatter
the back of the garment like a collection of bejewelled
brooches. Inspiration emerges from the intriguing markings
of moths, to create the rich textures of free machine
embroidery, goldwork, beading and gilded, foiled surfaces.

Observational drawings of hawk moths, together with
sampling, produced an elaborate, embossed effect with
stitch and appliqué. The winged fantasies emerge from an
intricate mix of gold threads, faceted beads, paillettes and
fine metallic cords. Hand and machine stitching intermingle
to create a lavish decoration. Techniques were inspired by
the wonderful medieval *opus anglicanum* embroideries and
the beautiful embellished Italian Renaissance velvets.